PYTHON

PROGRAMMING

FOR KIDS

Discover Tips and Tricks with this Parent and Teacher Friendly Guide for Kids

SIMON WEBER

TABLE OF CONTENTS

Introduction

The one thing that parents and guardians always strive to give their kids is a solid background and foundation for them to succeed in life.

Kids first learn their social environment and the ways to interact with people. As they advance in age, they begin to learn things cognitively. This is when they start to develop interests and life skills like art, math and - of course - tech stuff.

Parents and guardians can also shape the cognitive deductions of a child by the things they introduce them to. So, if you always have art around, or you never miss a day out at the art festival with your kid, there's a pretty good chance he/she will develop some interest in art.

It's the same with programming. The misconception about programming is that it should be left to the "geeks".

Programming is for uncool children who get bullied out of their lunch and run home crying, only to sit in front of a computer and code. Not true!

This is a common opinion that is wrong.

Teaching your children computer programming from such a young age will not only increase their general intelligence, but it is also the foundation that can and will build a career on.

Everywhere in the world, there's a huge demand for individuals who know how to code. In fact, in a recent online survey, it was found that the most lucrative skill in the world, at this moment, is computer programming and there are thousands of people who want to learn how to code every day.

If you've been following, you can see how important it is for your child to start learning how to code from a young age to secure a great future with a steady career.

And what better way to start than with Python.

The following are some of the benefits of coding that your kid will enjoy.

Benefits of Coding for Kids

1. Improved cognitive skills: By learning how to code, your kids will constantly embark on problem-solving experiences, which is what computer programming is all about.

In learning a programming language, the child is starting a skill that very few individuals from his/her age group will have. For this reason, the child will stand out amongst his or her peers.

2. Career opportunities: The world has gone completely digital and the best efforts we can make are to keep up with the pace. At the current pace, a programming language will soon be equally as important as our spoken and written languages.

Everywhere you go there is an opportunity for people who have computer skills and for people who can code. In the future, this current demand for tech skills will only rise, so it's a no-brainer for your kids to start to learn how to code at an early age.

3. Teaches kids emotional stability: From a young age, kids will understand the emotions of patience and perseverance - these are two things you absolutely need when you are coding.

The margin for error when writing codes is so small that one misplaced word or symbol could result in the entire program failing to run. In learning how to code, your kid will employ real-time emotions to achieve results.

4. *Kids may develop a passion:* There's nothing like starting a skill early that you grow to love and have a burning passion for. This is one of the biggest issues of the present generation. A lot of people are stuck in jobs that they are dissatisfied with because it doesn't spark their creativity and they have no real passion for it.

By starting to code from such a young age, your child may develop a passion for coding, and this sets them up for a career that they will enjoy and employment and the same time.

Digital technology will be a big part of the lives of your kids as they grow up. By learning how to code, your child will understand the mechanism of things around him or her.

This will spark their creative intuitiveness process and spark a skill that enables them to try and create similar or even better things.

Like learning a new language, it is important to utilize the brain of your children while they are still young and open to new information. It is a lot harder to start learning a new language with zero background when you are an adult.

As early as 7 years of age, your child will have developed enough cognitive and critical-thinking abilities that are required to learn how to code. By the time they are 10, they can create computer programs of high quality and that is of a professional standard.

The Man who wrote the Python Program

Amongst the many programming languages, Python stands out. According to John Edwards, a popular business technology journalist, his list of the programming language that is most in-demand in 2018, Python is second.

The man who wrote the Python computer programming language, Guido Van Rossum, announced that he wanted to write a code that was easy and could be understood in plain English. That was exactly what he designed - an intuitive text-based programming language that is easy to read and understand.

You've probably been wondering about the name: how did it come about? Well, it's kind of hilarious, really, but Van Rossum was reading the published scripts of a show on television named "Monty Python's Flying Circus" which he enjoyed.

He was looking for a name for the program he was writing, and he wanted something that sparked interest and was a bit of an enigma, so he chose 'Python'.

What is Python?

Let's start with what programming languages are - Programming languages are a series of instructions that are specially inputted into the computer for it to execute certain tasks. These instructions consist of syntax and semantics that are written in a way that the computer understands.

Python is a high-level programming language that emphasizes codes that are easy to read without too many complications.

This means that unlike in other programming languages where symbols like semicolon are used after statements, Python can simply use a space or a new line. This makes the program breathable and easy to understand and learn when you have no background knowledge of computer programming.

It is for this reason that it is extremely suitable for kids who want to learn how to code. Python's syntax is a lot less complicated than other programming languages.

Some lesser signs and symbols and codes make other programming languages a bit hectic and tiring. Python is readable but, make no mistake, it's just as effective. It is no wonder that it is so widely used by some of the biggest organizations in the world

Another thing that makes Python stand out is its standard library, which is very large and contains all the required tools to execute programs. The library consists of modules that Python uses to execute a large variety of tasks, and this is what makes it so unique.

With Python, almost everything has been simplified and stored in its library database with the Python code and all you need to do is to write certain commands that will initiate their functionality.

Python is incredibly versatile, and this is why it is one of the fastest-growing programming languages in the world. You can use Python to write simple programs in less than a minute and it can also create high-level entities like web, Internet, and software development and data analytics.

In scientific computing, Python has a large library that enables it to operate optimally. Some of them include Matplotlib, NumPy, and SciPy.

It has also had outstanding influence in fields like Architecture where it has been used to create design software like Autodesk Maya, 3Ds Max, Blender, etc.

Currently, according to different coding sources, Python is among the three most popular programming languages in the world - alongside Javascript and Java, making it one of the fastest-growing programming languages in the world.

The biggest organizations in the world use Python for coding every day. Giving your kid the opportunity to learn the language from a young age puts them on the path for a career with some the biggest names you can think of: Google (of course, even the author of the language worked at Google for 7 years), Facebook, Instagram, Spotify, Quora, Netflix, Reddit, etc.

Python is a programming language for the future. This is why your kid should get into it now. With Artificial intelligence and virtual reality earmarked to make a significant impact in the future, there's a lot to be done with Python.

In this book, your kid will learn Python programming in the most simplified way. The contents have been narrowed down bit by bit so that every detail is taken care of.

This book will teach your child how to learn Python. This is very important. It's not limited to what to learn, but how to learn a programming language that has grown with remarkable speed over the years.

It's important to learn Python so that your child understands the tenets and can begin to code on their own rather than simply dumping all the information onto their hands.

Make no mistake, as simple and easy to learn as the Python program is, it requires an attention to detail and a dedicated and interactive course to get through it smoothly. This is what the book offers.

From the syntax and semantics to the data structure, this book will take your kid on an interactive journey where he or she will learn how to code with Python without tears.

In order to optimize the learning capacity of your child by recognizing that he or she is in a delicate situation of learning something new and exciting, this book will pace the information it delivers by taking breaks and engage the kid on fun coding activities in between chapters and learning sessions.

The chapters, too, aren't just laid out. Instead, they follow a specific procession that aims to teach the child Python as if he or she is on a journey.

Each chapter builds upon the next. Like a sequence - you'll find out later on in the book just how important sequencing is when you are coding with Python.

If you miss one step, it could ruin the entire program. It's the same with the chapters. Every single one is important for the next stage.

Finally, you, as a parent or guardian, have a big role to play in your child's journey on learning how to code.

When reading the chapters of this book, the aim will always be clear that the author is determined to show the child just how much fun it can be to learn Python. We can all agree that when kids are doing something fun and enjoyable, they'll do it with so much enthusiasm and dedication.

In writing the chapters of this book, I hope that you will be determined to show your child how easy and enjoyable it is to learn Python.

Chapter One

Basics of Python Programming

You're here and ready to go, that's fantastic! This is the type of commitment that will soon help you create your first program. Are you excited about that? Yep, we are too.

But let's not get ahead of ourselves. In this chapter, you'll learn, first, the basics of Python, what it is, its components, and how to install and save it on your PC. It sounds like a lot, but it's as simple as counting popsicles. Let's show you how.

Learning the basics of Python is important on your journey to learn how Python programming language. It's like learning a new language in real-time. Before anything else, you must know the letters, how they sound, the vowels, alphabet structure, etc. Only then will you proceed to the more intricate aspects.

This chapter will break down the basics of Python programming language into diminutive fragments that are easily understood without any complications. This chapter will show you the things that are involved in creating a program on Python.

The explanation is clear and expressive, so you don't miss any bit of information.

When you've been supplied with a sufficient and thorough analysis of the components of Python, you'll move into a little more hands-on approach of using Python. It is here that you will create your first program and even go as far as looking at a solution to a real-time problem.

What are programming languages?

These are a kind of formal language that is used to communicate with the computer. Programming languages are simple instructions for a computer to carry out an instruction or a series of instructions.

The surface of a programming language is known as the syntax and can vary according to the different languages that are out there. Just as you would have with any other real-life language, programming languages make use of texts, symbols, punctuations, etc. to communicate with the computer.

The intricacy of how symbols and texts are used to form syntax is different, too, with the different programming languages. This is why it is easy to learn one from the other and why some of them are more popular than others. The implementation of the syntax and mode of execution differs too.

Python is a computer programming language that is popular because of its effectiveness, simplicity, and how easy it is to learn how to use it.

What Is Python Programming Language?

Python is a unique and high-level programming language that uses a very uncomplicated and straightforward syntax to create commands for the computer to execute a task or series of tasks. Also, Python is object-oriented with variables that are dynamically typed.

Let's take you through what this means.

Unlike most computer programming languages, with Python, you do not need to declare variables and individually write out the types.

This makes it incredibly easy and faster to create a code, especially for beginners.

Variables, data-types… do these sound new? You'll find out what they are soon. First, let's get your version of Python in and install.

Python 3

This is the latest version of Python and it's the version that almost every programmer in the tech world uses. According to numerous online surveys, Python 3 will completely wipe out the older version by 2020.

For obvious reasons, this is the version that you will be learning how to code with.

Let's look at a few of the benefits of Python 3 over the former version.

1. Newer Libraries are Incompatible with Python 2

The libraries being created by tech developers in recent times are only compatible with Python 3. To utilize the better and more efficient libraries, more company programmers are switching to Python 3.

2. Better Intelligence in Integer Divisions

One of the perks of Python 3 is how it uses intuitiveness to derive solutions. This is incredibly helpful for beginners who are just starting to learn how to code.

For example, in Python 2, when you make a simple division of two numbers, the result is rounded up to the nearest whole number even if there is a remainder.

If you type 4/2 on Python 2, the result will be 2. Accurate. However, if you type 7/2, the result will be 3. To get an accurate value, you'll have to input the whole numbers as decimal numbers. So, 7.0/2.0 will give you 3.5.

Python 3 makes it easier through intuitiveness to know that 7/2 will give you 3.5 so you don't need to write it as a decimal.

3. Python 3, by default, stores strings as Unicode

When using Unicode strings, you can store symbols, emojis, the letters of a foreign language, etc. This is a lot more expressive than in ASCII, which is where strings are saved in Python 2

4. More refined and Bug fixes.

Some of the problems that Python 2 runs into have been fixed in the newer version. It is now more refined.

By 2020, everyone would be using Python 3, so it wouldn't make so much sense to learn anything else.

Getting started with Python 3

Python 3 can run on a lot of operating systems like Windows, Linux, Ubuntu, Mac, etc.

Also, Python comes pre-installed in some of the operating systems. However, they are usually in the older versions.

Want to see what version of Python has come with your computer? Easy!

Open the Python terminal, it has a plain black interface, and input the following command

Python - V

Click enter and voila!

To get the best package, you will have to download Python 3.

The software can be downloaded on the PSF - Python Software Foundation website. Your operating system might also need an installer to run Python, depending on which one you use.

OS like Linux comes with a package manager that helps Python to run on the computer.

Since we do not know the type of Operating systems that your computer comes with, we will be looking at how to install Python on the most popular ones and also, wait for it, on Android. So, you can take Python with you on the go.

Python 3: Windows Installation

Step 1: Download

The Python latest version is available for download on the Python software foundation website at http://www.Python.org/

Move to the bottom of the site and choose the installer for Windows. You can choose from the Windows 32-bit installer or the 36-bit installer. There's a difference between the two, and it depends on your computer.

We are assuming you already know the processor bit system of your computer. If you don't, you can always check it out.

For a 32-bit processor, the 32-bit Windows installer should be chosen to run the Python program. If you're using a 64-bit processor system, though, you should maximize and go for the 64-bit installer.

Step 2: Run your chosen Installer

Once your installer is in, double-click on the downloaded file and a series of instructions will come up on the screen on how to install Python.

Listen to this information: it is important to select the system path that you want to store Python at this point. Tick the box that says "Add Python 3.7 (or any other Python 3 versions) to path".

Once this is done, click on Install and Python 3 will be fully installed on your system.

We are going to be doing a lot with the Python software, so let's get it on your desktop for easy access.

First, right-click your desktop with your mouse, then select a new shortcut. Add the location (like you did during the installation) and finish with a name for the shortcut. Easy.

Python 3 on Linux

Linux operating system always comes pre-installed with Python. Always. Only they are usually in Python 2 version, so there's the need for an upgrade to the latest version.

You can check out the existing version of Python on the system by opening the terminal and inputting the simple command

Python - - version

If that doesn't display anything, try out the next one

Python2 - - version

If your operating system has any version of Python 2 installed, it will indicate it here.

You could see a response as

Python 2 .5. 8

This is the version available on your computer.

Python3 - - version

This will reveal if your system has the latest versions of Python 3 or not. Since this is rarely the case, you'll have to download the latest version of Python. The Python software comes with a package manager on Linux, and you can simply download the latest version from here.

Python 3 installation on Mac OS X

Like, Linux, Mac comes pre-installed with the Python software. Also, it is usually an older version. To download the latest version, go to the Python software foundation website and download it for Mac.

You can choose from the two installers available for Mac, depending on the version available on your system.

For a system with Mac OS X version from 10.3 to 10.6, download the 32-bit installer. While for Mac OS X versions that are from 10.6 and above, the 64-bit installer is great.

After the file download, click on it to reveal a drop-down with the file contents. This is usually "Build.txt", "License.txt", "Python.mpkg", "Readme.txt".

Double click on "pytho.mpkg" and proceed to install the software. When you're done with this, you'll need to create a shortcut on the desktop.

Alternatively, and the best and most efficient method of installing Python for Mac OS X, is by installing Homebrew. Homebrew is a package manager that is used for installing Python 3.

Open your browser and load the page http://brew.sh/. Upon loading the page, a homebrew code will be displayed under the option to "Install Homebrew". Copy the entire text of the code and save it to your clipboard.

Next, open a Terminal.app window and paste the code got from the website. Click enter and watch the Homebrew package manager installation.

Hold on though, we're not quite there yet.

Homebrew will create a user account for you and ask you for a password before proceeding. Once entered, relevant files will be downloaded online (so you should have an internet connection), and the installation will be complete. Easy? You bet.

Python 3 Installation on Ubuntu

To download the latest version of Python on your Ubuntu operating system, click on the Ubuntu software center icon. At the top right corner of the software center page, input 'Python' into the search box.

A result of the installed Python software on the operating system will come up. Click on the IDLE with the highest version of Python. For example, if there are 'IDLE (using Python 2.7.7) and IDLE (using Python 3.5.8) versions, you must pick the one with the latest version and click install.

Before you authenticate the software, you will need to enter the administrative password of the system and then install it.

Python 3 for Android and iOS

There are mobile software applications that create a Python environment and allow you to practice Python on the go.

Pydroid 3 is an Android application that supports Python 3.6 while Pythonista is available on iOS play store for your iPad or iPhone.

Wow, that was a lot of information. How about a quick Python trick just to try out the new software we just installed? Ok, here we go.

Manipulation of Strings trick

For this magic trick, we need a volunteer. Yes, you are reading this. You'll do nicely.

What we need for this trick is a string.

Remember that we are in the programming world, so a string is different from the one in real life. A string, here, is simply defined as an arrangement of characters.

For example, the letter A - standing alone it's an ordinary variable, but when the letters r r o w are added, it becomes a string: a sequence of variables.

So how do you create a string in Python programming?

You can create a string by surrounding the variables with quotation marks.

When you open the Python shell, you'll see three greater-than signs (>>>). This is known as a prompt. So, don't be confused, it's there to help the program run.

Now for our magic trick. After the prompt, type *my_string = "I am excited to learn Python"*. (Remember to always close the quotation).

When you press enter, another prompt command comes up on another line. Type *Print (my_string) and run the program.*

I am excited to learn Python will be boldly displayed.

You can allocate variables to strings in programs so that you can easily use them. For example,

    a = "I am excited to learn how to code"

When you type print (a), the string is displayed, and when you are writing a long program anywhere the variable a is inputted; it stands for the letters in the string.

But that was just coding; it wasn't a trick!

After typing your print command

Print (my_string) and you add the mathematical operator * like this

*Print (my_string * 2)* and run, here's what will appear.

I am excited to learn how to code. I am excited to learn how to code.

Tada!

Congratulations on your first program. By no means an easy feat.

Save the program you just wrote

If you exit the Python software without saving the program you just wrote, you'll lose all the changes made on that program. Doesn't sound like a disaster? You just wrote an 8-word program! Think about a large program with so many lines and chains of command and imagine losing that sort of progress. It could be devastating.

This is why you must ensure that you save your program, and you can do that in a few steps. To save your program on Python, open IDLE and click File at the top left corner of the tab and then New window.

A blank window will pop up on your screen that will be tagged as untitled in the menu bar. Alternatively, you can just press CTRL + N and the new window will pop up and is tagged as *untitled.*

Input the command Print (my_string * 2)

Before the program can run, you need to save it. Click on File and then Save. After this, you will be asked for a filename under the Python directory .py.

Let's name the program Excited.py and save it on the desktop, where you can easily access it later.

Finally, under Run, select Run module and your program is safe and complete.

Phew, what a journey it's been so far. Let's take a look at all that you learned in chapter 1.

1. You learned the basics of Python programming language. Also, you learned the meaning of programming language and why Python is the most popular of the rest of them.

2. We also told you about the benefits Python 3 has over the older Python 2 and why it is important.

3. You didn't just stop there. You learned how to install Python on some of the operating systems.

4. Then you wrote your first program (we're still buzzing) and learned how to save your program file.

5. Finally, you practiced Python magic trick, and the result was exciting, am I right?

In chapter two, we'll go into calculation and variable in Python.

Right now, you need a break because you've been terrific so far.

Chapter Two

Calculations and Variables in Python

As you may have noticed, we need some math in everything we do, every day (try going 30 minutes without doing something math-ish or running numbers in your mind, it's almost impossible). If you're looking forward to the first thing to do with Python, why not try out something as simple as solving random mathematical calculations? Everyone sure wants a means of solving long and boring mathematical problems. Lucky enough for us, the computer beats our calculative minds in any mathematical equation that exists. It can perform over a billion (or as many as you can imagine) calculations in just a second! Python gives you mathematical computing power and lets you use a whole set of symbols to do math with different numbers.

Python Numbers: Are they different from regular numbers?

Because you want to ask our program to solve the right equations (because computer language isn't 100% human language), you need to know the basic types of numbers that exist in the Python language. The first is the *integers*. They are the regular whole numbers that we use when counting, doing basic math, or telling our age like 0, 1, 89, 20225, and negatives like -88. The other is the *floating-point numbers* or *floats* for short, which are the decimal numbers like 0.8, 2.0, and 7.888 used to describe fractions.

Basic Python Operators

When you want to make mathematical calculations, the most common operations you perform are addition, subtraction, multiplication, and division, right? Those basic symbols we use to represent this operation are what we call *operators* in Python. The + (plus), - (minus), * (multiply by), and / (divide) represent the effect and calculations we want our set of numbers to have in that particular equation. So, if you input 3*4, you want to multiply your first number 3 by 4, which gives you 12.

Less Basic Python Operators

With Python, you can go further and perform mathematical calculations that your basic calculators don't provide for you. They are the *exponent* and *modulus*. As technical as they may sound, they are pretty straightforward operations. Not to worry, the only reason they are referred to as 'less basic' is because they are not the regular ones you're exposed to. Imagine you have to multiply a particular number by itself a number of times, say multiply 5 by itself 6 times. You do this using the *exponent* operator, which is the double asterisk (**). Now instead of typing 5*5*5*5*5*5, you only have to type 5**6 and get the same answer. It is the same as when you have 5^6 in a math problem.

In regular math, when you divide integers by other integers (remember integers?) and the numbers don't divide evenly, you have a remainder. In Python, going through the normal division route doesn't show you what remainder is left. You only get the whole number answer. For instance, 5/2 gives you 2 in Python. In the actual sense, there's a remainder of 1. To fix this, Python provides a special operator that allows you to check the remainder of your division equation. We call it *modulus*. It's represented by the percent (%) symbol. So, to get the remainder of 5/2, you input 5%2 and get 1.

Order of Operations

Now that you understand the basic and not so basic operators that can be used when calculating with Python, you should also know that there's a particular order that the operators have to follow to get correct answers and program right. There's only one way you can input your different operators in whichever order you wish to have them and still get the right answer. But before going into that exception, it's important that you're reminded about the order that the math rule (and Python in turn) follows. It is exponent first, then multiplication and division, then addition and subtraction. So, if you input 2 + 2 * 4 into a Python program, you'll be getting 10. If your intention is for the program to add up 2 and 2 before multiplying the answer by 4 and get 16, you'll have to go a little mile further.

Here's where the exception we spoke about a few words ago comes in. You have the option of adding *parentheses* or *round brackets* as they're regularly called. The *parentheses* indicate that you want the operation inside the brackets to go first before the others follow. So, in this case, when you input (2+2)*4, you'll get 16 instead of the 10 when you carry out the operation without a round bracket. You can also have *parentheses* inside another *parentheses*. Say, ((5 + 10) * 20) / 10. With this, you're telling the computer to operate on the innermost bracket first, then go into the outer bracket, and then the rest of the equation according to the basic math rules. In this case, you get 30. This works because all the mathematical rules that you know apply to Python, and other programming languages.

Calculating in the Python Shell

You sure do know how to do regular calculations on pen and paper or on calculators. But how do you do math with Python? Here's how you go about it:

You start a Python shell by double-clicking the IDLE icon on your desktop. You get a >>> symbol which is the *command prompt* where you can input whatever it is you want your computer to process, which in this case is a math calculation. Try typing in a basic calculation like 7+6, and press ENTER. You should see the answer to your equation, which is 13.

You can also use the Python program to solve your daily mathematical problems, like knowing how much you'd need to save daily to achieve your goal of buying yourself a present at the end of the year. You can try this out on your own Python shell and see how much you should put into your piggy bank daily.

Remember, multiplication and division always go before addition and subtraction, unless parentheses are used to control the order of operations.

Variables in Python

Don't forget that Python is a language (of the many languages) that the computer understands. You can use this language to command the computer to do a lot of things for you, one of which is calculating your Grade 3 mathematics. Whether the computer is helping you calculate your homework or helping you build your dream game app, the computer is always collecting things and putting them into something we call a memory. Now, human beings have memories too. The things we see, hear, and feel are stored up somewhere in our brains. But the difference between our memories is that while there's a high chance we don't remember things accurately (we're not that perfect), a computer never forgets what has been stored in its memory. The only things that can be done to the things stored up in a computer's memory are to recall, replace, add to, subtract from or delete completely.

To make things easier for you to remember and tell the computer where exactly to put them in its memory, programming has what we call *variables*. A *variable* is likened to a container where you store up information such as numbers, texts, list of numbers and texts, and anything you want. Variables are like putting labels on things, so you'll know exactly what they contain when you need them. Imagine having a kitchen cabinet with many little identical porcelain jugs that contain different cooking ingredients. If there're no labels on them, you'll most likely have to go through (or taste in some cases) all of them to know which one is the salt or black pepper. But if they have correct labels already, you'll only have to pick the one you need, use and replace. It's that simple. That's how easy *variables* make your programming for you.

For example, to create a variable called **name**, we use an equal sign (=) and then tell Python what information the variable should be the label for. We create the variable **name** and tell Python that it labels the number 12.

To find out what value a variable labels, enter **print** in the shell, followed by the variable name in parentheses. Then, it gives you the output.

We can also tell Python to change the variable **name** so that it labels something else. For example, you can change the variable **name** to now contain 45.

Just to confirm the change, we can ask (using the **print** command) what **name** is labeling in the next line. Python will print the result on the last line.

The great thing about using variables is that you can use whatever labels you choose, as long as you can remember what they represent. Variable names can be made up of letters, numbers, and the underscore character (_), but they can't start with a number. You can use anything from single letters (such as X) to long sentences for variable names. (A variable can't contain a space, so use an underscore to separate the words). It's advisable to use short variable names when you're doing something quick. The name you choose should depend on how meaningful you need the variable name to be.

How to Use the Variables

Now that you know how to assign variables to different values, the next step is understanding how to use them right. Let's create a scenario running from a previous one of calculating how much you'll have to save daily to be able to buy yourself a present at the end of the year. Imagine at the end of the year, you're unable to save the exact amount of money to buy yourself the dream gift, but your dad, seeing your efforts, asks you for the amount left so he can add up to it to get you your gift.

You only have to use your Python shell and assign variables to calculate it. Let's see…

Amount_needed= $40

Amount_in_hand=$33.75

Since regular math makes us understand that you'd have to subtract the amount you have from the amount needed to know how much will be left, then you have…

Amount_left=Amount_needed – Amount_in_hand

We have assigned our chosen variables to the values we have. All we have to do next is to input this into the Python shell and **print** the answer you're looking to get (i.e. print Amount_left) and see the outcome it gives. Just in case your saving goals are the same as mine, you should get $6.25. This means that your dad is going to give you $6.25 extra. Remember that while calculating with Python, you don't need to include the units (miles, sheets, dollars, or $) they stand for, just the numbers.

In the case that you get to the store, and you find out that your dream present has increased to $43, you can still use the same variable, only that you'll change it to contain the new value. Here's how you can input it in your Python shell. On a new line, enter *Amount_needed= $43. Then,* copy and paste the equation to calculate the answer again, to give you:

Amount_left=Amount_needed – Amount_in_hand

Then, go ahead to **print** your new answer.

Strings

We already know how to communicate and get outputs (the results that you get from using the **print** function) in numbers. But what happens when you want to communicate in long sentences that have more words and texts than numbers? This is where *strings* come in.

When you hear strings, the first thing that may come to your mind are those thick metallic instruments on a guitar that produce sound. Those strings are a collection of thick metallic instruments that make up the guitar. In programming, also, *strings* are a collection of letters, texts, characters, symbols, and even numbers. Your name is a string; your home address is a string too. This entire book can be referred to as strings because it includes collections of letters, numbers, and different symbols.

In Python, creating a string is putting the word, words, numbers or characters in quotes. The quotes can either be double (" ") or single (' ').

You can assign variables to strings. That means you can have something like,

name= "Alice"

If you ask your computer to **print(*name*),** you get Alice has your output, without the quotes.

You can also choose to assign a long string to your variables. You can have,

> *name*= "My name is Alice"

You can **print(*name*)**, to see what is now inside the variable.

It is important to know that '11' and 11 are different from Python. The first is a string; the other is an integer (your regular whole number). Thus, you'll have to use them differently. But if you wish, you can convert a string to an integer, and vice versa. Python has the function of **int** that coverts an '11' string to 11. All you need to do is type the int function before the variable. Here's an example:

> age='11'

> print (int(age))

You'll now have a regular integer.

Same for integers to strings. All you have to do is input the **str** function before the variable. Here…

> age=11

> print(str(age))

Now, your former integer is now just a collection of characters (numbers in this case).

Errors and Problems with Strings

At this stage of writing codes for your computer, it's possible that you make errors if you don't follow the appropriate rules, especially when you're assigning strings into variables. If you enter more than one line of text for your string using only a single quote (') or double quote (") or you start with one type of quote and try to finish with another, you'll get an error message in the Python shell.

If you enter something like:

name= "My name is Alice

You'll get an error message because the computer can't understand what you're trying to ask it to do. You'll get a message like this:

SyntaxError: EOL while scanning string literal

This error message is complaining about the syntax because you did not follow the rules for ending a string with a single or double quote. *Syntax,* in this case, is simply the arrangement and order of words in a program.

SyntaxError means that you did something in an order Python was not expecting, or Python was expecting something that you missed. *EOL* means *end-of-line*, so the rest of the error message is telling you that Python hit the end of the line and did not find a double quote to close the string. For this line to be valid, you'll have to complete it with an ending quote.

You can use more than one line in your string. To indicate this, you'll have to use three single quotes, hit ENTER, then enter the rest of your string and close with three single quotes.

Lists

Variable can also contain lists. Usually, we use *lists* to keep a number of values that are separated by commas and put into square brackets []. You can fix any value type in lists, including numbers and strings. You can even have lists of lists. Let's have a list of your favorite colors and give its variable name as *favorite colors.*

27

In your Python shell, you'll input it as *favorite_colors*= ['red', 'blue', 'purple', 'green']. You then ask your computer to **print**(favorite_colors), and you get all the items on your list as [red, blue, purple, green].

You may be wondering what the list and a string is. A *list* has a number of features that a string doesn't have. It allows you to add, remove, or pick one or some of the characters in the list. Imagine over the next few years, you decide you have one more favorite color you want to add to your existing list, or you no longer like a particular color, a list in Python allows you manipulate it.

A string can't allow you to add or remove without changing the entire characters in it. We could print the second item in the favorite_colors (blue) by entering its position in the list (called the *index position*) inside square brackets ([]). *Index position* is the position the computer sees the items in the list as. To computers, index positions begin from 0 (instead of the regular 1 we're all used to). So, the first item on your list is in index position 0, the second item is in index position 1, and so on.

You'll enter something like, **print**(favorite_colors[1]) in your Python shell. You'll get blue after hitting ENTER.

To change an item in your existing list, you'll enter it this way:

favorite_colors[1]= 'yellow'

print(favorite_colors)

You'll now have:

['red', 'yellow', 'purple', 'green'] as your list.

You have successfully removed the item 'blue' and replaced it with 'yellow' at index position 1.

You may also wish to show only some part of your list. You do this by using a colon (:) inside square brackets. For example, enter the following in your command prompt to see the second and third items on your list.

>   print(color_list[1:3])

Writing [1:3] is the same as saying, 'show the items from index position 1 up to (but not including) index position 3' – or in other words, items 2 and 3. This process is called *slicing*.

You already know how to replace items in list and pick out some items in the list. The ***append*** function is used to add items to a list. A *function* is a chunk of code that tells Python to do something (you'll learn more about them later on).

In this case, ***append*** adds an item to the end of a list. It goes this way:

>   color_list.append('white')

>   **print(color_list)**

>   ['red', 'yellow', 'purple', 'green', 'white']

To remove items from a list, use the ***del*** command (short for *delete*). To remove the third item on your list, it's:

>   del color_list[2]

>   **print(color_list)**

>   ['red', 'yellow', 'green', 'white']

We can also join lists by adding them, just like adding numbers, using a plus (+) sign.

If your first list includes numbers 1 to 3, and your second list includes random words, you can join them as one list. Here's how:

second_list=['buckle', 'my', 'shoes']

print(first_list + second_list)

After hitting ENTER, you get:

[1, 2, 3, 'buckle', 'my', 'shoes']

Tuples

A *tuple* is likened to a list. Only that, it uses parentheses. It will look like this:

numbers= (1, 8, 5, 4)

print(numbers[2])

You'll get a 5 output.

The major difference between a list and a tuple is that a tuple cannot be changed once created. And, that's the reason why we use them. When you need a variable that has elements that shouldn't be changed, tuples are your best bet.

Maps

Strings, lists, and tuples are all a compilation of different things. The difference between them is the form they take. *Maps* are another collection of things. The difference is that a map (or *dictionary)* has a key and a corresponding value.

A good example of a map will be:

favorite_characters= {'Jane': 'Captain America', 'Danny': 'Thor', 'Toby': 'Iron Man', 'Gracie': 'Antman'}

The colons (:) are used to separate the key from their corresponding values. It's possible to make a list out of this example, but in the case that the elements are a lot more and you can't easily skim through to pick the one you want, then a map can come in handy.

To get Toby's favorite character, you'll do this:

> **print**(favorite_characters['Toby'])

You get Iron Man as your answer.

Maps are very useful when there's a long element list and you'll need to access some of them later on. They are enclosed in braces {} which is their major differentiator, along with the colon.

Maps are similar to lists and tuples in their functions, except that you can't join two maps together or you'll get an error message from the computer because Python wouldn't understand what you're commanding.

Chapter Three

What Happens IF...?

At this point, we've already gone through how to command our computer to give us the output we want based on the processing of the input given. But do you know it's also possible to allow the computer to decide what its output is going to be based on the different inputs we give it, by itself? Computers have the ability to assess information and make small decisions very quickly.

You may need to ask someone a question, and the answer you receive would determine the reply you give to that answer. Does that make any sense to you? Let's imagine you're the lifeguard at a local swimming pool, and a group of five kids come around with the intention to swim. Before they get in, you can ask them, "Are you all 16 and older?" If their answer is "yes", then you can say, "Okay, go in." But if they seem unsure or say "no", then you will say, "Sorry, children less than 16 are not allowed in here." This is because there's a standing rule that children less than 16 shouldn't be allowed to swim without adult supervision.

You can interact with your computer this way using Python! These kinds of questions asked are referred to as *conditions,* and we combine them with the responses into *if statements.* These statements can be used to build programs in Python. Here's how:

If Statements

The *if statement* is one of the most important programming tools. It allows you to tell the computer whether to run a group of instructions, based on a condition or set of conditions or not.

With an *if statement*, you're giving the computer the freedom to make its choice. In regular English, an *if statement* could be read as, "if this condition is true, do (print) this".

An *if statement* consists of the following:

The if keyword,

A condition (that is, a statement that can either be true or false),

A colon (:),

Starting on the next line, a block of code, which if the answer to the question is yes (or *true*), the commands in the block will be run.

Here's how you write an if statement in Python:

```
age=12

if age<16:

    print('Sorry, children less than 16 are not allowed in here')
```

Now you may be wondering what a block of code is. A *block* of code is a grouped set of programming statements. It is one or more lines of code that are grouped together. They're all related to a particular part of the program (like an *if statement*). In Python, blocks of code are formed by *indenting* the lines of code in the block. Indenting is a necessary part of how you write the code because it tells Python where blocks of code start and where they end. The *if statement* needs a block of code to tell them what to do. The block tells Python what to do *if* the condition is true.

Luckily for you, Python 3 automatically puts the indentation for you after you input your *if statement* (ending it with a colon) and hit ENTER. But in cases where you have really long lines of codes with different blocks, you may have to do some yourself. That's why it's necessary to master the indentation rules.

For our example above, you may want to go further than just print, "Sorry, children less than 16 are not allowed in here." Perhaps you want to print out other sentences to make your point concrete.

Here's how it's going to be arranged on the Python shell.

```
age=12

if age<16:

    print('Sorry, children less than 16 are not allowed in here')

    print('You should come with an adult next time')

    print('Or just wait till you're up to 16')
```

This block of code is made up of three print statements that are run only if the condition age < 16 is found to be true. Each line in the block has four spaces at the beginning when you compare it with the *if statement* above it.

A code that is at the same position (indented the same number of spaces from the left margin) is grouped into a block, and whenever you start a new line with more spaces than the previous one, you are starting a new block.

When you group statements together in a block, then you're trying to show your computer that they're related and that they should be run together. When you change the indentation (putting in more whitespaces), you're indicating that it's another group of statements that should be run differently from the previous. If your indentation doesn't align (have the same spaces), you get an *indentation error* from your computer.

You always have to remember that correct indentation determines how the computer interprets your code. You have to be consistent with your spacing. IDLE (the current version of the Python program) tries to help you with this indentation as much as it can.

Comparisons Operators

Remember the basic operators that we use to solve mathematical calculations? Well, there're certain symbols in Python that we can use to test and compare two values to see if the criteria set is True or False. You want to know if one value is bigger or smaller than the other or if they are equal? Here are the compassion operators:

  == Equal to

  != Not equal to

  > Greater than

  < Less than

  >= Greater than or equal to

  <= Less than or equal to

The single equal sign is already used as the assignment operator. So, if you input x=25, you mean to say that you're assigning the value 5 to the variable x. But if you input x==25, you mean that x *is equal to* 5. They mean different things.

To test if two values are not equal, you use the != operator. If you're trying to test if x *is not equal to* 25, you input it as x!=25.

For easy understanding, you should try out some examples on your Python shell.

Let's set x with the value 25.

```
x=25.

if x==25:

    print('x is a perfect square')
```

You should have a x is a perfect square outcome.

However, if you input it this way:

```
if x<25:

    print('x can do better')
```

Because the conditional statement is not true, your computer will not carry out any command, and therefore give you an empty output. You'll have nothing printed.

But if you have:

```
if x>=25:

    print('we're not sure where x stands')
```

The computer will carry out your command because the conditional statement is true (although x isn't greater than 25, it's equal to 25).

The computer is going to carry out (print) your command when the statement in the condition is true. What happens when the condition is false, but you still want your computer to do (print) something? This leads us to the If-then-Else statements.

If-Then-Else Statements

This type of statement in real English is really just saying, 'if something is true, then do this; or else, do that'. Here's an example:

```
x=25

if x<10:

    print('x is such a little number')

else:

    print('x can do better')
```

What do you think the outcome will be? Because the conditional statement is false, it wouldn't print the first message. Then, you've commanded that it prints the second message in the case that the condition is false. Thus, your outcome will be the second message.

You can also have this:

```
x=25

if x>=21:

    print('x has a lot of potential')

else:

    print('x keeps getting better')
```

If you guessed (before inputting it into your Python shell, of course) that it'll give you the first message, then you're correct! Because the conditional statement (x is greater or equal to 21) is correct, it'll print the first message and ignore the second. The second message can only be considered when the conditional statement is false. Else statements can only come after an if statement or elif statement(s). What's an elif statement, you may ask…

If and Elif Statements

There's really no limit to what you can do with conditional statements. If statements can be extended to elif (shortened form of else-if) statements. What you're literally saying to your computer is 'if this is true, then do this. Else if this other statement is true, do this…'. You can always have more than one elif in the same statement.

You can also combine them with an else statement, which can **only** come after the elif statement(s) has been inputted. Let's set x to value 25 again.

x=25

if x==16:

    print('x is the square of 4')

elif x>67:

    print('x')

elif x<=11:

    print('x is x')

elif x>20:

    print('x is greater than 20')

else:

    print('x has to make up its mind')

Here, the computer first checks to see if the conditional statement is true. If it's true it follows the first print command. If it's not (which it actually isn't) the computer skips the command and jumps to the next statement and checks for its truth value. If it's true, it prints. If it isn't, it skips and jumps to the next statement. The computer keeps doing this until it finds a statement amongst the if statements that are true, then prints its message. If it turns out that all the if statements are untrue, it goes ahead to print the else message like it has been taught to do. And if there's no else statement, it does nothing and gives an empty output. But if one of the many if (if and elifs in this case) statements turns out to be true, it ignores the rest (including the last else statement) and prints the message of the true statement.

Combining Complex Conditions

In the case that you don't want really long and complicated codes, you can combine conditions by using the keywords (which will be elaborated later on) *and* and *or* instead. Here's how:

```
x=25

if x==10 or x<12 or x>20:

    print('x can be a lot of things at the same time')

else:

    print('x is king!')
```

What this implies is that the computer will carefully look into the conditional statement that has three different conditions, and check to see if one or more is true.

If two of the three are false, but at least one is true, it automatically makes the entire statement true. And because of this, it prints the first message and ignores the else statement. But if all the conditions turn out to be false, it ignores (totally) the first command and prints the else statement's message.

We can also have:

```
x=25

if x<30 and x>=20:

    print('x is undaunted!')

else:

    print('no more x')
```

Here, the *and* keyword in the conditional statement implies that both (or everyone if there are more than two) conditions have to be true for the entire statement to be true. So, if both conditions (x being less than 30 and x being greater or equal to 20) are true, the computer prints the first command and ignores the else statement. But if at least one is false, the entire conditional statement becomes false despite one of the conditions being true. Thus, it skips the first print command and follows the second print command.

Variables with no values-NONE

We already learned that we can assign whatever we wish into a label (called variable in Python, you know this). And whatever here can actually include nothing; an empty value. In Python, an empty value is called None.

```
x=None
```

When you ask your computer to print x, you get None as your output.

You may set a variable to None if you know you're going to need it later, but still want to define all your variables from the onset.

Tips 'N' Tricks

- *if statements* are only executed when the particular condition is true.

- **True** and **False** are called Boolean operators. Whenever they're used, the statement is either automatically true or false. Remember, always type the words starting with block letters so the computer can identify what you're trying to use it for.

Chapter Four

Let's Talk About Loops

One of the reasons we use computers in the first place is because we want to do things easily and reduce tediousness. One of the ways that activities get quite tedious is when we have to do the same thing over and over again. Who wouldn't wish for a magic wand to help us do something we've already done once, again, whenever we need it? Python presents to us this magic wand in the form of *loops.*

Loops repeat the same steps (blocks of code) or things like other programming statements automatically. There're two types of loops that perform different functions. The first is the *for loop,* which repeats and counts a certain number of times. The other is the conditional loop, which continues to repeat until a certain thing happens. It's referred to as the *while loop* because it continues to repeat itself as long as the condition is true.

Using for Loops

With what you've learned so far, if you want to repeat a line of code 4 times, you'll have to print it 4 times, this way…

```
x=4

print(x)

x=4

print(x)
```

```
x=4

print(x)

x=4

print(x)
```

An easier way of doing this is for you to use for loops. It'll go this way...

```
for x in range(1,5):

    print(4)
```

OR

```
for x in [1, 2, 3, 4]:

    print(4)
```

Not to worry, we'll explain. For the first option, the *range* is another function (there're a bunch, and we'll discuss them better later on) in Python (that's why the color is a bit different from the other ones) that allows you create a list (remember lists?) of numbers from the starting number up to the number before the ending number.

You're literally telling the computer that you need a list of the numbers from the starting number (which in this case is 1) up to the number just before the ending number (which is 5) here. Range uses regular numbers, not index positions. The range function doesn't create lists. It doesn't have the power to that on its own. But when combined with a loop, it returns an iteration (each time it goes through the loop). Here's what you're commanding the computer to do with your code:

- Start counting from 1 and stop just right before 5.

- x here is just a variable (the label we've decided to use. It could be anything). For each number we count, store its value in the variable x.

- Then, print the message 4.

When you hit ENTER, Python prints the message four times. There're four values stored in the variable x four times. That's why your output is 4, four times.

For the second option, here's the interpretation:

- There's a list of numbers from 1 to 4. The variable x then starts with the first number in the list and stores it as 1.

- The loop follows the command of the next line (instruction to print) one time for the value 1 in variable x.

- Then, it comes back to the next element of the list, which is 2, and stores it as 2. Then follows the next line and prints the message. It goes back until it exhausts the elements on your list.

Your list can include anything from numbers to strings. You can decide to have:

```
for x in 'You are doing great':

    print(x)
```

Your answer should like this:

```
Y
```

o

u

a

r

e

d

o

i

n

g

g

r

e

a

t

If you're surprised at the spaces, there's a perfect explanation. We already concluded that strings are a collection of characters, numbers and/or letters. These characters include everything between the opening quote and the closing quote –including *whitespaces.*

What happens when you want to have contracted words like don't or wouldn't in your strings, or you want to have quotes in your string? Python allows us the alternative of using three quotes (either single or double) at the beginning and end with three quotes (either single or double) at the end. Here are some examples.

x= '''you're doing great'''

print(x)

y= '''She said, ''you're doing great, Tammy''''''

print(y)

When you run this, the output is:

you're doing great

She said, "you're doing great, Tammy"

You'll notice that the second input had three single quotes at the beginning of the string, and had a double quote opening and closing the quotes contained in the string, before ending with three single quotes. Yes, that's how it works with Python. If you begin and end your string with double quotes, then the quote in the string will have single quotes instead. One will have to give way for the other because you cannot have two different sets of double or single quotes in a string. Sounds complicated, but it's really straightforward when you try on your Python shell. It doesn't matter if there's a contracted form in the inside quote or not.

So, if you want to do a for loop for this, here's what your output will look like:

for x in '''You're doing great''':

print(x)

Y

o

u

'

r

e

d

o

i

n

g

g

r

e

a

t

The apostrophe is included this time!

You can print whatever message you wish.

A loop variable is the same as other variables. Just because it's in a loop doesn't make it different. It's just a label for a particular value, so you'd be able to recall from the computer memory.

The range function

This function is very useful while looping. It is possible that you don't give range() two numbers as we did earlier. You can give it just one number.

for k in range(6):

print(k)

Here, it would do the same thing as:

for k in range(0,6):

print(k)

And give you the list of numbers as:

0

1

2

3

4

5

The list begins with 0 because Python is programmed to start from 0. So, if you want it to begin from 1 or something else, you'll have to input the right number of the range's upper limit.

You may ask, "what if I want the loop to count in two, three, or twenty steps instead of the regular one? Or what if I want it to count backward?". Good news, it's possible. Try this:

for x in range(0, 10, 2):

print(x)

Ordinarily, you should get the list of numbers between 0 and 9 (because 10 isn't included). But because of the third number in the range bracket (called a parameter), the loop is now counting in steps of 2. So you first get 0, (skip one number, then the next), 2, (skip one number, then the next), 4, (skip one number, then the next), 6, (skip one number, then the next), 8, (skip one number, then the next), and nothing else because the loop has been completed.

Something similar will happen if you use a parameter of 3. It'll give you 0, (skip two numbers, then the next), 3, (skip two numbers, then the next), 6, and continue till the loop is completed.

When you need to count backward, your range limit is switched (instead of front to back, you'll have back to front). Your parameter is also in the negative. Here's a visual representation:

```
for x in range(10, 1, -1):

    print(x)
```

When the third parameter is in the negative, the loop counts down. And because the loop will start from the first and ends just before the second number, your output will end at 2, not 1.

Looping over Strings

For loops save us the stress of repeating lines of codes. It comes in really handy when you have to write long lines of codes.

For loops can also be used when you've already created a list of things to set them into a variable. If you need the content of that list, all you need to do is *for loop* it. Here's how:

```
favorite_colors= ['red', 'yellow', 'purple', 'green']

for a in favorite_colors:

    print(a)
```

You get all the items on your list printed. Easy-peasy.

You can also have:

favorite_colors= ['red', 'yellow', 'purple', 'green']

for a in favorite_colors:

print(a, 'is my favorite color')

Here, in addition to the list of your favorite colors, you're able to indicate to someone who doesn't bother to read your code but only sees the output that what you've run are actually your favorite colors. You've asked your computer to print a string of message that serves as an indicator. It makes it way easier for your code to be understood. You don't need to put your variable in quotes again. The reason the value is put in a variable is so you can 'call on it' anytime you need it without stress. Note that there's a comma (,) inside the print statement. The function of the comma is to separate the already stated variable from the string you inserted. You can also insert commas to separate different variables in a print command. Commas are used to separate different data types (strings, integers) and variables so the computer can interpret right.

Remember that Python always expects the indentation (number of spaces in a block) to be consistent. IDLE automatically indents for you, but you can alter by mistakenly inputting your DEL, TAB or SPACE buttons. When this happens, you get an *indentation error,* and Python cannot interpret your command until you correct it. Plus, correct indentation makes it easier for humans who check out your code to understand.

You can do a lot of exciting activities with for loops. You can complete your multiplication tables. All you need to do is apply the rules in the right way.

Here's how:

```
for x in range(1,13):

    print(x, 'times 5=', x*5)
```

To explain, you want a multiplication table of 5 from 1 up to 12. So, your range starts from 1 up to the number before 13. The command is that for every value in the variable x (from 1 to 12 that is), print the value x, and the string times 5= and the value of x multiplied by 5. The string is printed literally, and the other values are automatically processed by the computer.

With correct indentation, your output should like this:

1 times 5= 5

2 times 5= 10

3 times 5= 15

4 times 5= 20

5 times 5= 25

6 times 5= 30

7 times 5= 35

8 times 5= 40

9 times 5= 45

10 times 5= 50

11 times 5= 55

12 times 5= 60

Conditional Loops

There're times when you may not know how many times you'll need to run a loop, or even have no list of value to use. For these cases, a for loop may not be all that useful. But there's another type of loop that can be employed. It's the conditional loop referred to as the *while loop.* If you want a loop that runs until something happens and you're not when exactly that'll happen, you can use a while loop for these.

From what we learned from if statements (telling your computer to run a group of instructions or not based on a condition or set of conditions set), instead of counting how many times to run a loop, you can use a condition (test) to decide when to stop a loop. A while loop keeps looping while some condition is met. It stops looping when a condition is no longer true. Just as for is the keyword for counting loops, while is the keyword for conditional loops.

A simple while loop will be:

```
x=10

while x==10:

    print('I cannot stop!!!')
```

What happens when you hit the ENTER key? You get an unending loop of 'I cannot stop!!!'. This is because the conditional statement is true, and will always be true. So, the loops keep coming back, over and over again to check if it's true, and if it finds it true (which it always will), it'll keep printing your message. And this will continue until you do something. The easiest step to stop this unending loop is the CTRL+C way. Press down the two keys at the same time, and it interrupts it immediately.

In addition, there are times when you'll want the user to make the inputs himself. In cases when you're building apps, games, or websites, to ease interactions between the computer and the users, the users will have to enter their inputs, which will then determine the next action that the computer will take. Let's see how that'll turn out:

```
name=input('What is your name?:')

print(name)
```

What happens when you process this code? The computer gives you a 'What is your name?' block that actually wants you to enter your name! This is possible because of the input function we have in the code. It allows the user to input whatever he wants in line with the request, even after the command has been carried out. Awesome right? You may or may not include the colon as it is there. The colon just aids the user to be absolutely sure the computer is asking him to input something.

At this point, you can include a while loop statement to make it more meaningful. Let's try it out.

```
name=input('What is your name?:')

print(name)

while name== 'Tammy':

    print('Welcome, Tammy')

if name!= 'Tammy':

    print('This is not your computer')
```

Want to guess what the outcome will be? It first off asks you for your name. The name you input will determine the next action of the computer. You'll notice that we've introduced an if statement into this while loop. Yes. This is possible because they are both based on the condition. An if statement's command will execute if the statement is true. A while loop will keep looping as long as the condition is true. Here's what the computer interprets the rest of the code to be:

- When you enter your name and it isn't 'Tammy', it prints, 'This is not your computer'. Just once, because it has crossed to an if condition.

- But if you type your name and with some luck it turns out to be 'Tammy', then the while loop statement is true; thus, it'll keep looping the print command until you decide to do something about it (like interrupt it). In this case, you've given the computer two different commands to carry out. Although it cannot do both at the same time, it'll at least do one because the statement is either true or false. And your code as provided for the two possibilities.

Don't forget the block rules. The if statement is aligning with the while loop because it's stemming from it.

Let's try to go even further.

```
print("Hi, Tammy. Type your passcode to proceed, anything else to quit.")

passcode=input()

while passcode == "password":

    print("""You're right. That's your passcode.""")

    print("""That's not right, I'm quitting now.""")
```

This code asks for input from the user. It can be interpreted as while the passcode is equal to password and the condition is true, it keeps looping over and over. But if the passcode is not equal to password, then the condition is false. Only then does the loop stop and prints the last message.

Sometimes, you may want to break out of an unending loop. There are two ways this can happen. Either you jump ahead to the next iteration of the loop, or just stop looping all together.

Continue- Jumping Ahead

A loop can contain different iterations. You may want to stop executing the iteration you're on at the moment and move on to the next one. The way to do this is with a *continue* statement. Let's have an example:

```
for x in range(0,8):

    print('This is Us')

    if x>3:

        continue

    print('This is not us')
```

You should get this output:

```
This is Us

This is not Us

This is Us

This is not Us

This is Us

This is not Us

This is Us
```

This is not Us

This is Us

This is Us

This is Us

Here, the first four times, because x is not greater than 3, it jumps to the next message in the loop. The fifth time through the loop when x is greater than 3 for the first time, the rest of the loop didn't continue. Instead, it jumped ahead to the next iteration and prints the first message till the end of the statement. This is exactly what continue statements look to do in loops – whether while or for loops.

Break- Jumping Out Completely

In some cases, you may decide to break out of the loop completely and avoid the end of the condition in all. Here's where the **break** statement comes in. Let's have the same code as we did for the continue statement and only replace the continue with break. When we input it, here's the output you should get:

```
for x in range(0,8):

    print('This is Us')

    if x>3:

        break

    print('This is not us')
```

You should get this output:

This is Us

This is not Us

This is Us

This is not Us

This is Us

This is not Us

This is Us

This is not Us

This is Us

The outcome is, the first four times the loop runs because the value of x is not greater than 3, it goes ahead to print the next statement. But as soon as it reaches the fourth time, which is greater than 3, the loop stops.

Let's try it again, this time with a while loop.

```
for x in range(0,8):

    while x<6:

        print('HERE IT IS')

        break
```

The result you get here is, it prints your message, just six times. Without the break statement, it would be an endless loop. The break sentence is saying, "in the range of 0 to 8, for the times that x is less than 6, print this message. And after that, jump out of the loop. If there was another statement after this, it would have gone ahead to process it.

Tips 'N' Tricks

- Although *for* loops and while loops are similar, they're used to mean different things. The *for* is used when you know the particular length you have to reach, *while* is used when you don't know.

Chapter Five

Drawing with Python

In the last chapters, we've learned how to count with Python, how to put names and data types into variables, how to do our math homework with Python, and so on. A lot of people may be looking forward to the part where we begin to build our own games (don't worry, it'll definitely come). But there's yet another amazing thing we can do with Python. And that's to draw. You can command Python to draw lines, shapes, and even a bit further than that.

The module (you'll learn about this later on) in Python that allows you draw lines and shapes is referred to as the *turtle*. The turtle is just like its name in actual life. It's a small black arrow that appears on the Python screen that moves around quite slowly and leaves a trail behind it. If you're looking to learn basic computer graphics, then Turtle is the right platform for you to use.

Using Python's Turtle Module

The turtle module is a way through which you can direct graphics by drawing dots, lines, and curves in your program. Here's how Turtle works. Once you start the Python shell on your computer, you'll need to ask Python to import the turtle module from its memory by typing this into the interactive shell:

>>> import turtle

Now you've told Python you want to use it, and it's understood the command. Next, is to create a canvas.

Creating a Canvas

A canvas is a blank space to draw on. To create one, you'll have to call the *Pen* function from the Turtle module. Here's how it goes into your Python shell:

>>> t = turtle.Pen()

After doing this, you should get the canvas (an entirely different blank box) that has a little black arrow at its center. The arrow you see there is the turtle. So, your turtle is ready and down for work. The rest of it is in your hands.

Moving the Turtle

The variable name t that you created earlier is what you'll use to send a message to our drawing friend, the turtle. There're a couple of other specific functions that are embedded in the module, and t is what we'll use to send the specific messages. Say we want our turtle to advance (to the right, since that's where it faces by default) 100 pixels forward, we do this:

>>> t.forward(100)

The arrow gets longer! By 100 pixels that is. Up next, you can command the turtle to go 90degrees. Here's how:

>>> t.left(90)

You turn turtle left and right by angle units. When the turtle turns left, it rotates around to face the new direction. The t.left(90) command points the arrow up (because it started by pointing to the right).

With what we've had already, we may decide to add more code lines and draw a square with turtle. Here,

>>> t.forward(100)

```
>>> t.left(90)

>>> t.forward(100)

>>> t.left(90)

>>> t.forward(100)

>>> t.left(90)
```

With this, you should get a 'perfect' square.

But in the case that you make a mistake while drawing (like I did while I was trying out mine) or you just want to restart, there's a function in the module called the reset function that erases everything for you. Here's how:

```
>>> t.reset()
```

It resets it to its original position. The other alternative available is:

```
>>>t.clear()
```

This one clears, but still leaves in the current position. Let's try out some of the many functions.

```
>>> t.backward(120)

>>> t.up()

>>> t.right(90)

>>> t.forward(20)

>>> t.left(90)

>>> t.down()

>>> t.forward(120)
```

This will give you two parallel lines. Here's how and why:

The Python turtle is already reset to its original position. The t.backward(120) now moves the turtle backward 120 pixels. Then the t.up() picks up the pen and tells Python to stop drawing. Then, with t.right(90), you turn the turtle right 90 degrees to point down toward the bottom of the screen, and with t.forward(20), you move forward 20 pixels. Turtle just turns but doesn't draw because of the up command already used. You turn the turtle left 90 degrees again to face right with t.left(90), and then with the down command, Turtle knows it's time to put the pen back down and continue drawing. The final thing it does is to draw a line forward, just like the first line we drew, with t.forward(120). The two lines are parallel to each other with some distance between them.

You can now use Python's turtle module to draw simple lines, shapes and how to combine and turn by degrees, simple right? It would be great for you to know you can do even more complex graphics with turtle. You can draw more shapes, create and fill your shapes with color.

In chapter 3, you got introduced to different kinds of loops and how to use them. We can combine our idea of loops with that of turtle graphics. Here's how:

```
>>>t.reset()

>>> for x in range(1, 5):

    t.forward(100)

    t.left(90)
```

The reset function already puts the turtle back in its original state. Then, we initiate a for loop that counts from 1 to 4 within the code range (remember this rule?). The following lines, in each run of the loop, we move forward 100 pixels and turn left 90 degrees four times. The for loop we use here makes the code shorter and faster. Programmers, as a matter of fact, always look for the easiest and shortest ways to put down their codes. Why go 8 lines when in 4 lines you can write all you need?

With a little change to our last code, we can create something different with turtle. Here's how:

>>> t.reset()

>>> for x in range(1, 9):

    t.forward(100)

    t.left(225)

You should get an eight-point star. This happens because, first, your code loops 8 times. And every single time it loops, it moves 100 pixels forward, and then turns 225 degrees left.

You can extend the points of your star as much you want:

>>> t.reset()

>>> for x in range(1, 61):

    t.forward(150)

    t.left(175)

The functions in the turtle module can be combined with other features of Python (like loops and conditional statements) to get the outcomes we're looking to get. As long as they follow the rules, they'll produce dots, shapes, and lines of different kinds. But what if you want to combine lines, shapes, and a lot more in one program? Like draw a car? Let's see…

import turtle

```
t=turtle.Pen()
t.color(1,1,0)
t.begin_fill()
t.forward(100)
t.left(90)
t.forward(20)
t.left(90)
t.forward(20)
t.right(90)
t.forward(20)
t.left(90)
t.forward(60)
t.left(90)
t.forward(20)
t.right(90)
t.forward(20)
t.left(90)
t.forward(20)
t.end_fill()
t.color(0,0,0)
t.up()
t.forward(10)
t.down()
t.begin_fill()
t.circle(10)
```

```
t.end_fill()

t.setheading(0)

t.up()

t.forward(90)

t.right(90)

t.forward(10)

t.setheading(0)

t.begin_fill()

t.down()

t.circle(10)

t.end_fill()
```

You should get a yellow old regular jalopy from this code. This code includes a couple of turtle module functions like:

- *color-* can change the color of the pen, and everything it draws will be in that color.

- *begin_fill* and *end_fill* fill the area of the canvas with the color you pick.

- *circle* draws a circle for you.

- *setheading* allows the turtle to face a particular direction.

Coloring Things

The color parameter has three parameters. The first states the amount of red; the second the amount of green; and the third the amount of blue. For example, to get the yellow color of the car, we used color(1,1,0), which tells the turtle to use 100% of the red and 100% of the green pen.

The computer uses the RGB color recipe when combining colors. How you to combine the ration determines the outcome you get. To get a purple fill, you'll need 100% red, 100% blue, and no green.

Drawing and Filling Circles

We can move on to drawing a circle and filling it with colors. Here's how:

```
>>> def filledCircle(red, green, blue):

t.color(red, green, blue)

t.begin_fill()

t.circle(100)

t.end_fill()


>>> filledCircle(0, 0, 0.5)
```

Here, we've reduced the intensity of the blue color to 0.5 (50%), so you'll get a light blue circle. This shows that the color you get depends on which of the colors on the palette you use or how you mix them. You may get pink, purple, different shades of green or whatever you want. You only have to mix the color ratio!

You may decide you want a neutral color (black or white) circle or shape too. Although the color palette on our computer only gives 3 bright colors, the way you combine them, again, will determine the outcome. Using the same code as above (including the reset line of course), except changing the color ratio to filledCircle(0, 0, 0), you'll get a black circle. The ratio means, no red, no blue, no green.

If you need a white circle, Python's turtle module allows you combine the colors with the same ration like filledCircle(1, 1, 1) to get a white circle.

We've already drawn circles with turtle and filled them in. We already drew a colored car too. But what if you need to draw and fill up a square? Here's how:

```
>>>def mySquare(size):
    for x in range(1, 5):
        t.forward(size)
        t.left(90)


>>> mySquare(50)
>>> mySquare(75)
>>> mySquare(100)
>>> mySquare(125)
>>> mySquare(150)
```

This code gives you a couple of squares that keep getting bigger by 25 degrees.

To draw and fill a square, you only have to combine the two tricks you already know. Combine the drawing and filling functions, like this:

```
>>> t.reset()
>>> t.begin_fill()
>>> mySquare(50)
>>> t.end_fill()
```

We can now go ahead to create a function that allows us to have filled and unfilled squares. It's a little more complicated code, but you can always try it.

```
>>> def mySquare(size, filled):

if filled == True:

t.begin_fill()

for x in range(1, 5):

t.forward(size)

t.left(90)

if filled == True:

t.end_fill()
```

What this code interprets as is we first define our function to have the parameters, size and filled. Then we used a conditional statement that checks if the value of filled is equal to True. If it's true, then turtle knows to fill the shape we drew. It loops four times, which gives us a square then goes back to check again if the statement is still True. If it is, the color filling ends, and we get a square filled with color.

We can go ahead to draw a square with this line.

```
>>> mySquare(50, True)

>>> mySquare(150, False)
```

For turtle graphics, it goes as far as your imagination can take you. You can think up anything and decide to represent it on the Python turtle graphics. For better understanding, you can pick some of the earlier codes we wrote and fill them up with colors. Let's improve on the first star we drew and fill it in as an example.

```
>>> t.reset()
>>> for x in range(1,19):
        t.forward(100)
        if x %2 == 0:
            t.left(175)
        else:
            t.left(225)
```

The loop runs 18 times, and for those 18 times, it moves forward a 100 pixel. The introduced conditional statement checks if the variable x contains an even number through the modulus operator. It's literally asking for the left over when the number in the variable has been divided into two equal halves. The turtle then turns left a whole 175 degrees whenever variable x is even. Or else, it turns 225 degrees. You get an actual 9 point star. To fill it up:

```
>>> def myStar(size, filled):
if filled == True:
t.begin_fill()
for x in range(1, 19):
t.forward(size)
if x % 2 == 0:
t.left(175)
else:
t.left(225)
if filled == True:
```

t.end_fill()

>>> t.color(0.5, 0, 0.7)

>>> myStar(120, True)

The outcome is a 9 point purple star.

PYGAME, some help please...?

There's a means through which our drawings and graphics can be made a lot easier. Undeniably, using graphics can be a bit complicated with Python, there's a useful module that exists. It's called the Pygame module, and t lets you create the things that'll make your game work on any kind of computer or Python operator, like graphics and colors.

It is free to download and install. If you don't have it already, head on to the Pygame website, **www.pygame.org** and download it right away. Later on in this book, when we'll be exploring fun and games, we'll discuss extensively on Pygames. But for now, let's open our Pygame window and see how it works.

```
import pygame
pygame.init()
screen = pygame.display.set_mode([640, 480])
running = True
while running:
    for event in pygame.event.get():
        if event.type == pygame.QUIT:
            running = False
pygame.quit()
```

When you run this code, you should get a pygame window that opens on its own. Because the Pygame is meant to make games, there's a need to interact with the player so the name can know what to do. The event loop that is seen in the code is distinct to the Pygame module alone, and it's constantly checking that the user does something. It may be moving the cursor, pressing keys, or just closing the window. The Pygame program can't work without having the event loop running every time. The way to do this is to use a statement that keeps the computer on its heels every time. We know what that is. It's the while loop. The computer keeps running and looping as long the user is still playing the game. The only way of closing the program is to use the **X** button on the top right corner of the window. If you use a MacOS, you do this by closing the button on the top left corner. This is because the Pygame program doesn't include a menu. The code we have used above leaves the program open. The code you run in the screen variable is what determines the size of the window. It is 640 pixels wide by 480 pixels high.

The rest of the Pygame gist will be left for chapters 10 and 11 when we talk extensively on creating and programming games. Until then…

Tips 'N' Tricks

- Not to worry, you'll understand what *modules, functions,* and some other terms mean better in a couple of chapters from now.

- A pixel is a single dot on the screen of the computer. Everything you see on your computer monitor is made up of tiny, square dots. Every word, every letter, every icon, and every picture are made of pixels. It is the contracted form of 'picture element'.

- Don't forget to reset when your canvas is clustered!

- The trick to understanding how turtle (and most of programming actually) is constant practice. To aid your understanding, you should try do draw some of these shapes with turtle.

  1. A hexagon. You can use the rules we've gone through while drawing stars, squares, and rectangles to draw this 6- sided shape.

  2. You can go further than drawing the shape by filling it in with a color.

  3. You can draw a star like we've done before. But this time around, you use two parameters instead of the usual one.

  >>> def draw_star(size, points):

- You can also think of different ways of using the turtle module.

Chapter Six

Graphical User Interface

Up until now, every interaction we've been having with our computer has been all letters and numbers. You may have been wondering why we weren't having graphics and windows and buttons like you've known computers to have. If you've followed through so far, then it's time you get introduced to these graphical features. They're referred to as Graphical User Interface. It simply means that instead of sending written messages to the computers and getting the same back, you (or the user) sees windows, buttons, and lots of graphics.

What's a GUI?

Rather than saying Graphical User Interface all the time, you may just say GUI. When compared to the type of programs we've had so far, they're the graphical and fancier versions of our text mode or command line programs. They still do the same things as our previous programs. They have inputs, computer processes them, and gives us the outputs.

As a matter of fact, you have been using GUIs all along without knowing. Whenever you use a browser, you're already using a GUI. The Python IDLE window we've been using is actually a GUI. Just like Python allows you to create your own functions, modules, and a lot more, you can make your own GUIs also. There's a feature on Python that allows you to create your own GUIs. It's the **easygui.py** module. You, however, need to install the EasyGui first. Here's how.

First, go straight to **easygui.sourceforge.net/** and download the module. It's either you download it straight, or you download a zip file that contains the **easygui.py.** You also need to put the file in a place where you (and Python) can see it. The best path to put it is where the original Python file has been installed. Go to your hard drive and find the place and folder where Python has been installed and put the easygui.py there. Now you're ready to start using your GUIs!

Using Your GUI

Remember, we said that GUIs work when we send the message through our IDLE window first, and the user sees it through GUI? Well, to use GUIs, you'll have to start on your IDLE window. Here's how.

>>> import easygui

If you don't get an error message after this, well done, you've successfully installed your EasyGui module. You can now create a simple message box.

>>> easygui.msgbox("Hey, there!")

The msgbox () function helps create a message box. A message box is a box, with a message. You should get your message printed with an **OK** box. When you click the **OK** box, it closes.

But in case you don't want to use the IDLE window for your input, and you want to do it all on the GUI, then you can.

With the previous input, after you clicked the **OK** button and it closes, you get a message on your Python shell that shows you that the user already clicked the **OK** button. It's part of the module. To make it easier, you can put the response into a variable. This way:

>>> the_response = easygui.msgbox("Hey, there!")

So, if you click OK and print (the_response), you'll get the OK.

Dialog Boxes

The message box function you use is one of the many dialog boxes that the EasyGui provides for you. The dialog boxes are used to have dialogs with the user. You can tell the user something, or get some information from them. They vary from button clicks to string messages or even filenames. Your program can even include more than one button clicks. Let's create a dialog box that asks the user for her favorite color. The type of dialog box we'll use is the buttonbox.

```
import easygui

color = easygui.buttonbox("What is your favorite color?",

choices = ['Red', 'Green', 'Pink'] )

easygui.msgbox ("You picked " + color)
```

Once you save the file, you can run it. You get the options on your GUI immediately. You're asked for your favorite color. Whichever one you pick, you'll get a "You picked Red" (if you picked red) as your output. When you click the OK button, you'll get the same message you got on the other hand. If you cancel the program, you'll get an error message back. The computer expects that you pick one of all the options.

Text Input

In the case that any of the options you made available doesn't match the user's color taste, you can allow the user to input her choice with texts. The dialog responsible for this is the enterbox. Here's how it's going to look:

```
import easygui
```

color = easygui.enterbox("What is your favorite color flavor?")

easygui.msgbox ("You entered " + color)

On the GUI, you get a space to input whatever you want. After you type it in, you should click OK to continue. After this, it displays your input in the message box.

Default Input

Default inputs are used when a certain input is expected from the user. The default input doesn't mean that if the user doesn't input what's put on default, you'll get an error message, it's just to make using the GUI easier for the user. The enterbox dialog box is also used here. Here's how.

import easygui

color = easygui.enterbox("What is your favorite color?",

default = 'Red')

easygui.msgbox ("You entered " + color)

When you run this program, you get Red on the enter box. If your choice color isn't red, you can delete it and input your own color.

Using Numbers

The enter box allows you input strings, but if you need to enter numbers, you'll need to use the int() and float()to create them. The integer int() allows you to enter whole numbers. You can also decide to put a limit or range to the numbers that can be entered. The float float()allows you to enter decimal numbers. Float converts the number you input into the enter box as a string. Let's do this!

76

```
import random, easygui

secret = random.randint(1, 50)

guess = 0

tries = 0
```

easygui.msgbox("""You have to pick a random number between 1 and 50. If you pick the right number, you get your gift! You've 6 tries. Good luck!""")

```
    while guess != secret and tries < 6:

    guess = easygui.integerbox(""""What's the guess?"""")

    if not guess: break

    if guess < secret:

    easygui.msgbox(str(guess) + " is too low, try again.")

    elif guess > secret:

    easygui.msgbox(str(guess) + " is too high, go lower")

    tries = tries + 1

    if guess == secret:

    easygui.msgbox("You got it! Congratulations! You get a gift, soon!")

    else:

    easygui.msgbox("No more guesses, no more gifts. The right number was " + str(secret))
```

We've combined some of the functions we've learned so far to use this GUI. When you run this program, you should first get a message box asking you to pick a random number between 1 and 50 that can get you a gift if it's the right number. The random.randit() built-in function allows the computer to pick a random number (integer) between 1 and 50 itself. It's the computer that generates the number itself, not even the person writing the code. So, if you're lucky enough to guess the number that the computer has picked, the computer prints out the 'if' message. But if you're not able to get it right for the 6 guesses you get, the 'else' message prints and the program ends.

Other Available GUIs- PyQt

Asides, the boxes we've already used, there're other ones available. The choice box, for instance, allows you to pick different choices instead of one alone amongst the choices you get. So, you can use it for the previous program to pick two or more of the favorite color options you get.

But then, you may want to be in more control of how your GUI looks and make it more flexible. We'll introduce the **PyQt** module for this.

The first step is to download and install the PyQt program into your computer. **www.riverbankcomputing.com/software/pyqt/download** is where you can download this module from. As long as you get the correct version that works with your version of Python. To write Graphical User Interfaces, there're two main parts. First off, the User Interface itself has to be created. Then, to make it function and do what you want, you need to write a code to do that. With PyQt, the Qt designer is used to create the User Interface.

The PyQt program is useful because modern computers today need more than just dialogs.

Tips 'N' Tricks

- You may expect that GUI is pronounced letter by letter as regular abbreviations are. But it may be surprising to know that amongst programmers, it's pronounced as a word –gooey.

- Programmers don't always know everything that Python contains. There's a built-in help system in Python that helps you find out more about anything you ant. For the EasyGui for instance, you may type in:

  >>>help()

  Then, you type in anything to get more information. For the message box function in the EayGui module,

  >>>help> easygui.msgbox

  To get out of it,

  help> quit

  >>>

Chapter Seven

Functions and Modules

So far, you may have been wondering how you just type in some words into the Python shell, and they automatically perform an act (and usually have a different color) in your code. You may be wondering how print and input automatically carry out what you ask them to do. There's a good explanation for this. These features and words are called *functions.*

Programs always look for a way to make codes easier to keep and call out whenever we need them. Functions are a way to make this work. The little blocks of codes we've been writing so far are nothing compared to how much codes and lines of code we can write in one particular program. You may soon have to write longer and more complicated codes. And, we'd need a way to organize them in simpler and smaller pieces so we can write and reuse them whenever we have to. Who doesn't want to be able to command the computer to do what he wants whenever he wants?

Functions allow you to refer to those smaller pieces later in our programs by a single command or short name. It's essential to know how they work and call them whenever we need them. If anyone asks you what a function is, you can simply say "they're chunks of code that tell Python to do something". There're a couple of ways to reuse codes, and functions are one of those ways.

Parts of a Function

In the previous chapter, we used the range function to make Python count and the print function to make Python produce any message we input. But what exactly do they contain that make them work? A function has three components: a *name*, *parameters*, and a *body*.

Creating a Function

You *define or create* a function with Python's **def** keyword. You then use or *call* the function by using its name. Here's a simple example of creating a function.

```
def try_this_out(your_name):

    print('hello,', your_name)
```

Calling a Function

Calling a function means running the code that is inside the function. If you define a function with the def keyword but never call it, that code will never run. You call a function by using its name and a set of parentheses. Sometimes there's something in the parentheses and sometimes not.

For the first function we created, the name of this function is try_this_out. It has just one parameter, your_name, and its body is the block of code immediately following the line beginning with def (short for define). A *parameter* is a variable that exists only while a function is being used. You can run the function by calling its name, using parentheses (round brackets) around the parameter value like this:

```
>>>try_this_out('Tammy')
```

What you get is, hello, Tammy.

You can also decide to have more than one parameter.

```
def try_this_out(your_first_name, your_last_name):

    print('hello,', your_first_name, your_last_name)
```

Did you notice that once you type in your function, Python is already reminding you of the parameters in your function? That's how much Python wants you to get your program right. Another reason why using functions is important is that you are allowed to make them behave differently each time it you run them. It's called passing an argument into a function. Here's how.

```
def printMyName(mySurname):

    print(mySurname)

    print("Tamara")

    print("Phoebe")

    print("Kimberly")

    print()

printMyName("Blaise")
```

After running, you get:

Blaise

Tamara

Phoebe

Kimberly

The output is different every time the function is called. The name keeps changing because we *pass* the function a different name each time.

It's also possible to create some variables first and then call the function with them like this:

>>> your_first_name = 'Tammy'

>>> your_last_name = 'Johnson'

>>> try_this_out(your_first_name, your_last_name)

Another really popular function used is the return function. It literally allows you to return a value using a return statement. Here's one:

```
def distance_covered(on_bus,on_tricycle,on_foot):

    return on_bus+ on_tricycle+ on_foot

print(distance_covered(12, 15, 5))
```

Variable and Scopes

A variable that's inside the body of a function can't be used again when the function has finished running. This is because its *scope* exists only inside the function. Python's *memory management* makes sure this happens automatically. It uses the variables inside the function, and after it's done with them, it deletes them from its memory. They no longer exist. Here's how it works:

```
def distance_covered():

    on_bus= 12

    on_tricycle= 15

    on_foot= 5

    return on_bus + on_tricycle + on_foot

print(distance_covered())
```

Printing this returns the value of the total distance covered. You can't, however, pick a variable in the function that has already finished running to check its value or do anything with it. You may check it out to see. You'll definitely get an error message.

But if the variable is defined outside the function, it has a different scope. The part of your program where the variable is used is called its *scope*.

Here's one:

```
uncovered_distance= 3

def distance_covered():

    on_bus= 12

    on_tricycle= 15

    on_foot= 5

    return  on_bus  +  on_tricycle  +  on_foot  -
uncovered_distance

print(distance_covered())

print(uncovered_distance)
```

You'll see that the uncovered_distance variable still works in the function even though it isn't defined inside it.

The distance_covered(), on_bus, on_tricycle, and on_foot are called *local variables*. The uncovered_distance variable becomes a *global variable*. That is the exact reason it works in the function, even if it wasn't defined in it.

Modules

Asides functions, another way of collecting and reusing codes is through the **modules** keyword. Functions can also be grouped together into modules. *Modules* are smaller pieces that are used when grouping functions, variables, and other things together into larger, more powerful programs. They're the pieces of a bigger program. Each module becomes a separate file on your computer memory. You can take a big program and split it up into more than one module or file. Or you can start with one small module and keep adding pieces to make a big program. Whichever way you choose, some modules are already built in to Python, and you can download other modules separately. Modules are useful because:

- It is easier to find things in your code.

- You can use a module in this program and adopt it again while on another program.

Modules are particularly useful when writing and building game codes. You can also use them to draw three-dimensional graphics.

If functions are like building blocks, then modules are the blocks that you use in building. These blocks are not scattered everywhere, they are put in little containers.

Let's Create Modules...

Creating a module is just like creating a Python file. You type the code you want to save as a module into the IDLE Python shell and save it as you'll wish. Let's have an example.

```
def kg_to_ton(kilogram):

        ton= kilogram * 1000

        return ton
```

Immediately after this, you only have to save this module as you'd wish. You can save it as test_modules.py. That's really all you need to do to create a module.

How then do you use these modules?

You create modules so you can call and recall them in other programs when you need them. So, if you're writing codes in a program and you need to convert a particular kilogram to tons, all you'll do is use the import keyword to call on your module, like this:

import test_modules

You'll be able to use the functions in the modules as you want. But so as not to confuse Python, you may need to be more specific in telling Python about how you're defining the functions in other modules. So, you may use something like this instead:

ton= my.module.kilogram * 1000

Namespaces

Using functions and modules require that you understand what namespaces are and how to use them. To get the hang of this, let's use an illustration. You have a brother named Danny. If your Mom or anyone around wants to call his attention, they'd probably just say, "Hey, Danny, come over here". But imagine you both have to go on a vacation with some of your friends and cousins. And it turns out you have a cousin who bears Danny too. There's going to be a little bit of difficulty when you have to call either of them, right? If you want to call your own brother, you may say something like "Danny, my brother..." and for your cousin, you my say, "Cousin Danny..." When you're home without your cousins and someone calls 'Danny', you know they're referring to your brother. But when you're with your cousins, and someone says just 'Danny', both of them are likely to answer. So, in relation to programming, in the *space* of your home, you have just one 'Danny'. Your home is your *namespace,* and therein, there's just one Danny, so no one is confused.

At the beach (for vacation), if you don't want to differentiate which Danny when calling, you'll probably walk over to the Danny you're referring to and say, "Hey, Danny". In programming, your home (a smaller namespace) will be referred to as the *local namespace,* and the beach will be the *global namespace.*

Importing Namespaces

Importing from a module means that you have access to every name (variable, object, and functions) in that model. Importing a module is like importing a namespace. So, if the name "Danny" is contained in the namespace of your home, importing it will be like importing the module from your home.

There're two ways through which you can import a module (namespace). First:

import Danny

This is easily imported because you have direct access to the namespace without having to indicate which 'Danny' you're referring to.

But imagine while you all are on your way home from vacation, a neighbor of yours (Jesse) who was on vacation elsewhere has to join your bus home. In programming, it's like bringing another *local namespace* into an existing *namespace.* If you want to import this new neighbor from the module, you'll have to go the extra mile. You'll have something like this:

import New_Neighbor

Take_home(New_Neighbor.Jesse)

Only when you do this will you be able to call out the specific name you need.

Importing Using from.

The other way to import is by using the keyword *from*.

from New_Neighbor import Jesse

If it's done this way, the name Jesse gets included in your New_Neigbor namespace. All you need to do is "take Jesse home".

Take_home(Jesse)

In the case that you have picked up more people like Jesse, and you've included them in the New_Neighbor module, and you're taking them all home,

from New_Neighbor import *

The asterisk here signifies 'all'.

Standard Modules

It's great that you now know how to create and use your own modules. But you don't always have to write your own modules. Python comes with certain built-in modules that you can call and use whenever you need them. They allow you to do things like find files, generate random numbers, or even tell the time. These, and much more, are regarded to as the *Python Standard Library*. They're a group of modules on their own. Functions like *print, if, else* and *elif* are basic commands in Python that are not categorized in any module (you don't have to import or import from anywhere as you may have noticed so far). You can hardly use Python without using these keywords – they're already a part of Python itself.

So you know, Python doesn't contain all the modules you'll ever need. You may be thinking that you'll just create them for yourselves, which is a good idea. But there're some modules you can just download add-on modules from the Internet.

Here're some of the built-in modules in Python.

Time

If you ever need to calculate the current date or time, the *time* module allows you to get the information from your computer. It's simply:

```
import time
```

The command here tells Python that we want to use the module time. This module also has functions in it that can be called using the dot (.) symbol.

The current date and time can be called with the asctime function. Let' see how.

```
import time

print(time.asctime())
```

You get your current date and time with this function!

Ever thought about slowing down your program runs? Python presents a built-in function that allows you to delay the program for a while. It's the *sleep ()* function, which allows the program to sleep for a while (you decide how many seconds you want it to sleep for). Here's how it works.

```
import time

print("How")
```

```
time.sleep(4)

print("are")

time.sleep(2)

print("you")

time.sleep(2)

print("today?")
```

Using the sleep () function cannot work without importing the time module. This is because sleep isn't a part of the main program's namespace. So whenever you want to call on the sleep () function, you'll have to call the time function first as time.sleep().

You may also ask Python to look for a function named sleep in the built-in time module, then include it in your namespace. Here's how.

```
from time import sleep

print("'I'll text you in 4 seconds..'")

sleep(4)

print('Hey, there...')
```

If you don't know the variables in the module you'll eventually use, and you don't want to specify the module name every time, you can use the asterisk (*) to import all names in your namespace.

```
from time import *
```

The * means *all*, so it imports all the names from the module. This is a little tricky, though. Creating two similar names in the program and in the time module will lead to a conflict. Importing from the module with * may not always be the best way to do it. You can just import the parts you need alone.

Random Numbers

You may want to build apps or even games that need you to generate random numbers. Python, once again, presents a built-in module that allows you to generate random numbers. It's the random module. Here's an example.

```
import random

print (random.randint(0, 50))

print (random.randint(0, 50))
```

The .randint() represents a random integer, and every time you use it, you get a new random integer.

If you need to get a random decimal number too, you'll need the random.random(). Here…

```
print (random.random())
```

Without anything in the bracket, you get random decimals between 0 and 1. But if you need random decimals between 1 and 10, you multiply your result by 10. Here's how…

```
print (random.random()) * 10
```

File Input and Output

The modules and their functions, amongst other computer inputs, are stored somewhere. That's why the computer can remember them when we need them. Remember in chapter 2, when we spoke about the computer memory, that's the place where all these 'memories' are stored. While some are stored in Python (the built-in functions and modules that we'll discuss later on), some others are stored in some particular file. As it ever happened that you were wandering around in your computer, you come upon some files hidden somewhere in your computer, and when you open them, you can't seem to understand them? Some of those files could belong to Python and its many entities. These 'weird' files usually consist of programs of games or apps. Every interaction you have with your apps and games are stored up somewhere where you can recall them (mostly unconsciously) whenever you need them. Or how else did you think your computer is able to save up your games and all your high scores even when your computer goes off abruptly? These programs are able to get their input from a *file* saved up on the computer's hard drive.

Asides **functions** and **modules,** there's another feature of Python that the computer automatically knows what to do about it and doesn't fall under the function and modules category. There's a part of the computer's *documentation* that are called *comments*. There're times that you may have to add notes into your codes to help you, and any other person looks in through it understand what you did. These comments work the way regular comments work. The computer ignores them when you write them and doesn't run them.

There're a couple of ways you can add comments into your program. Here are the ways.

Single Line Comments

The simple way of adding a comment to a program is to use the hashtag (or pound sign or number sign character) at the beginning of the line. Here's how.

This is how a comment works

If you run this program, you get nothing.

Then, if you add another line of actual code, your computer ignores your comment line and processes the next line. Add this line to your line of code.

print("The comment line was skipped")

When you rerun this code, the computer goes ahead to print your message, having skipped your comment line.

End of Line Comments

The other way of adding comments to a program is including those comments at the end of the code line. Like this:

current year – current age # this is how you get your date of birth

Everything before the # is regarded as a code, and everything else after it is a comment.

Multiline Comments

You can have more than one comment line in your code.

****

The row of stars is used to visually separate the comments

from the rest of the code

****

Triple Quoted Strings

Using triple quoted strings aren't really comments, but they act as one. Earlier in the first chapters, we learned that quoting words puts them into a string (a collection of characters). Using triple quotes is for the times when there's a quote or contracted form inside your string. But, you can use triple quotes to indicate a comment too. Since the string doesn't have a variable, and the computer isn't commanded to do anything, it just displays it the way it is and 'pretends' to be a comment. Here's one.

>>> """ A triple quoted string can be used

as a comment, although it isn't

really a comment.

It only pretends to be one.

"""

So when you see this in your program, you know what it is. This type of comment is rarely used by programmers, as it's just easy to # your comment in your program!

Comments also have their own special color – red. But when you use the triple quoted strings as comments, there's no red color. It shows up as blue when printed.

Why Comments and How Should They Be Used?

Comments are important because you can't always remember everything. Imagine you're writing a code, and you have to go to school. If you put in a comment or many comments, you understand what you've been doing and what you've trying to get to when you read your comments. Even the most skilled programmers use comments.

What you put into your comments totally depends on you. It's better to write them in a way you'll understand when you're back to it. After all, your computer isn't bothered by it. You finally get something in Python that works based on your own rules.

Commenting Out

Commenting out is another way of using comments. You can write codes that you don't need the computer to process yet, but still process the ones after. Take the input() function and loops for instance. While writing your code, you may want to check if some parts of it work. But you don't need an infinite code to keep running. You simply input a # to temporarily comment the line out until you're ready to run the entire program. Here's an example.

print("what does it mean to comment out?")

#print("You can always uncomment me whenever you want")

print("that's what happened in the previous line")

The first line gets printed, the second ignored, the third printed. You can always come back to uncomment it by simply removing the hashtag. In case you have extremely long lines of code and you have commented out a lot of them, going through it one by one can be quite stressful. Luckily, most code editors, including IDLE, allow you automatically uncomment some lines quickly. They're usually found in the **Format** menu.

Tips 'N' Tricks

- Sometimes, it isn't easy to identify which variables are local or global. And, this could make your code more confusing because you could have different variables having the same name. This is fixable. Just use different names for the local and global variables. This way there's hardly any confusion.

- You can't have numbers starting variable names. They must begin with either a letter or an underscore character.

After this, you can use the letters, numbers or characters anyhow you wish.

- Spaces are not allowed in variable names.

- The letters can be a mixture of lower cases and upper cases.

- You have to remember that cases matter. Da in Python is different from da.

- Documentation is the information about a program that describes it and how it works. There are many parts to documentation and comments are just one part. The help function that was mentioned earlier is a part of the program's documentation. It helps programmers figure out some things they don't already know about Python.

Chapter Eight

Using Classes and Objects

So far, we've seen that Python largely depends on the organization and collection of data. From lists, which are a collection of variables, to functions, which are a collection of collecting codes together so you can call or recall them whenever you need them. Modules also stem from functions, as a collection of these functions. There's another form of classification referred to as *objects.* Being able to collect functions and variables (data) together is the reason why objects exist. It's yet an easier way to classify your codes into smaller things, which eventually build up into a complex idea.

To understand this better, here's a simple illustration. If you're asked to think up two random things, you'll come up with the most random things, but we'll use book and puppy for now. Go a further step by trying to think about these two objects. What are they? Describe them as much as you can. For the puppy, you'll probably use terms like, 'animal, 'living thing', 'smaller dog', etc. For the book, you'll probable say that it's an inanimate object, and the color it has.

Using the terms 'animal', 'animate objects', 'smaller dog', is the way of classifying the things you've listed.

You may hear programmers say "Python is object oriented'. The object they refer to here is the many many collection of codes and variables together. The fun thing about objects is that they're quite easy to use, and although you can, you don't as a matter of necessity have to create them yourself. We'll now to ahead to learn what they're, how you can create and use them.

Objects in Python

Random things such as books are regarded as 'objects'. The things you know about these things like size, color, etc are the attributes (and are usually in variables). The things you can do with these objects are referred to as the methods. For you to easily remember:

Thing = *object*

Features of thing = *attribute*

Things you can do with the thing = *methods*

Using our first example – book –,

Book = object

Color, size, weight, number of pages = attributes

Read, write, open = methods

Now let's see how these will look in a Python interactive shell

book.color

book.size

book.weight

book.page_number

book.read()

book.write()

book.flip()

When displaying the attributes:

print book.color

When assigning values to them:

book.color = black

When assigning them to regular, non-object variables:

myColor = book.color

When assigning them to attributes in other objects:

myBook.color = yourBook.color

Objects are essentially made up of attributes and methods. You're collecting the things you know about the things and what they can do together in one place.

This may just be the perfect time to explain what the dot (.) is representing in the codes you've been writing. It's referred to as the *dot notation* and it's needed when you want to use the attributes and methods of the objects. We may now go ahead to learn to create this object.

Creating Objects in Python

There're two things to be done when creating objects.

First off, you need to describe how the object will look and act like. It's like putting together the blueprint for a project. The blueprint makes you understand the features (attributes) and how it can work (methods) of the thing you're trying to build, even before it's created. That's exactly how it works in programming. The blueprint you create for your object is referred to as the *class*. Once the class has been created, then you move on to the next step.

Creating the object with its blueprint (class) is the next step. If you think about it that's how things in life work. You want to build a house, you put up a blueprint first. Then you use the blueprint to build the actual car. It helps you understand how to go about the building and reaching your goal. You're creating an object at the *instance* of that class. If we want to create a class for our example above, here's how it'll look:

```
class Book:

    def flip(self):

        if self.direction == 'left':

            self.direction = 'right'
```

Here, we've defined the book with once method flip(). Attribute, however, can't be created this way because they don't really belong in a class. Rather, they belong to each instance. All attributes will belong to different instances.

Creating an Instance of an Object

Since we already have a class now, we'll go ahead to create an instance of an object from it. For the instance of Book, we do it this way:

```
myBook = Book()
```

Our book has no attributes yet, so we'll give it some:

```
myBook.direction = "right"
```

myBook.direction = "left"

myBook.color = "black"

myBook.size = "large"

There's another way of defining attributes in an object, but we'll be exploring that as we go on.

Now that we've defined attributes, we can go ahead to try out some of the methods. Let's use the flip () method:

myBook.flip()

You can go ahead to input it in the Python interactive shell and print them to see the outcome.

```
class Book:

    def flip(self):

        if self.direction == 'left':

            self.direction = 'right'



myBook= Book()

myBook.direction = "right"

myBook.direction = "left"

myBook.color = "black"

myBook.size = "large"
```

```
print("I just bought a book.")

print("My book is", myBook.size)

print("My book is", myBook.color)

print("My book flips to the", myBook.direction)

print("Now I'll flip the book again")

print

myBook.flips()

print "Now the book's flipped to the", myBook.direction
```

The code above should give you:

I just bought a book.

My book is large

My book is black

My book flips to the left

Now I'm going to flip the book again

Now the book's flipped to the right

The flip() method when called the first time flips the book to the left and later changes the **direction** from **left** to right. That is exactly what the code in the flip () method was created to do.

Python's 'Magic' Methods

Initializing an Object (_init_ method)

There's a special method that can be used to run the code whenever you create a new instance of the class you have defined. This method is called the **_init_()** that creates the instance with the properties set whichever way you want. Here's how to go about it:

```
class Book:

    def _init_ (self, color, size, direction):

        self.color = color

        self.size = size

        self.direction = direction


    def flip(self):

        if self.direction == 'left':

            self.direction = 'right'


myBook= Book("black", "large", "left")

print("I just bought a book.")


print("My book is", myBook.size)

print("My book is", myBook.color)

print("My book flips to the", myBook.direction)
```

print("Now I'll flip the book again")

print

myBook.flips()

print "Now the book's flipped to the", myBook.direction

If done correctly, you'll get the same output as the last code. The only difference is that you use the initialization (_init_) method to run the instances defined in your object class.

The _str_ Method

This method tells Python what to show when you **print** an object. There's an existing _str_ method in all Python objects. If you don't create yours, the already existing one is what Python is going to use by default in printing your object. But if you want to display something else with your print function, you can define your own _str_ and will override the default one. In the simplest terms, this method changes how the object prints. Let's see an example.

```
class Book:
def __init__(self, color, size, direction):
self.color = color
self.size = size
self.direction = direction
def __str__(self):
msg = "Check out my new book. It is " + self.size + " " +
self.color"
return msg
myBook = Book("black", "large", "left")
print myBook
```

After running your program, you should get:

Check out my new book. It is large and black

What's Self and Why Are We Using It?

While naming class attributes and method definitions, the word 'self' came up a couple of times. You may be wondering if it's some sort of built-in function that you've not been told about. In the real sense of it, a blueprint (class) can be used to build more than one house (object). So in the case that this happens, you'll need a way of telling the method in the class which of the different objects as called it.

The self-argument here is referred to as the *instance reference.* You should know, though, that the name **self really** has no specific meaning in programming. It just happens that over time, programmers have been using as their instance reference that nobody bothered to use any other variable again. It's one of those conventions that became a rule. You're not going to get penalized if you don't decide to follow the 'Programmers tradition' though. You can use absolutely any variable you wish for your instance reference. But since you already started with the self instance reference, it would be easier to continue with it. Plus, it gives you one less confusion when you begin to write long, complicated codes.

The information about the instance reference is automatically passed on to the method when you call a class method.

Now, you'll need to put in all you have learned on objects and classes into use. Let's use (paint) an Art work as the example.

First off, what do we do? We draw up the blueprint with the attributes and methods.

- finish_level. This is used to determine how long we've been painting for and how far the painting as materialized. We'll use numbers to represent – 0-4 hours for starting up, more than 4 hours for half-way through, and over 9 hours for a finished artwork. Anything more than 12 will be a distortion of art.

- finish_string. An actual string that describes how finished your artwork is.

- paint(). This is the method. You paint for a period of time to finish your work.

- We'll also use the _int_ and _str_ special methods to create your class instances and set them to default properties. The _str_ makes your print look even nicer.

Now that we've drawn up the blueprint, we can go ahead to define them in the Python interactive shell. Let's get to it!

```
class ArtWork:

    def __init__(self):

        self.finish_level = 0



        self.finish_string = "Empty"
```

Now we create a method and add some attributes:

```
    def paint(self, time):

        self.finish_level = self.finish_level + time

        if self.finish_level > 12:

            self.finish_string = "Distorted"

        elif self.finish_level > 9:

            self.finish_string = "Perfectly finished"
```

```
        elif self.finish_level > 4:

            self.finish_string = "Half-way done"

        else:

            self.finish_string = "Empty"

    myPiece = ArtWork()

    print(myPiece.finish_level)

    print(myPiece.finish_string)
```

Noticed that we brought in conditional statements into the code we're writing, it's because every part of coding is intertwined. It's important that you understand the basis of every aspect and how you can use them. Back to our ArtWork program, what the code above is interpreted as is:

We need to define how long it would take to finish painting this artwork. The finish level increases by the number of hours (time) you spend painting. If you paint for more than 12 hours, you'll have a distorted artwork. Else, if you paint for more than 9 hours (but not more than 12), you'll have a perfectly finished artwork. Else if you spend more than 4 hours but not up to 9 on your painting, you've only gone half-way. Else, then you still have an empty artwork.

If we run this, all we get is:

```
    >>>

    0

    Empty
```

We can now test out paint() method.

```
    print("""Now, I'm going to start painting my artwork""")
```

```
myPiece.paint(6)

print(myPiece.finish_level)

print(myPiece.finish_string)
```

>>>

0

Empty

Now, I'm going to start painting my artwork

6

Half-way done

We can add the _str_ method and test everything all together.

```
class ArtWork:

    def __init__(self):

        self.finish_level = 0

        self.finish_string = "Empty"

    def __str__(self):

        msg = "artwork"

        msg = msg.strip(", ")

        msg = self.finish_string + " " + msg + "."

        return msg
```

```python
    def paint(self, time):
        self.finish_level = self.finish_level + time
        if self.finish_level > 12:
            self.finish_string = "Distorted"
        elif self.finish_level > 9:
            self.finish_string = "Perfectly finished"
        elif self.finish_level > 4:
            self.finish_string = "Half-way done"
        else:
            self.finish_string = "Empty"


myPiece = ArtWork()
print(myPiece)
print("Painting artwork for 6 hours...")
myPiece.paint(6)
print(myPiece)
print("Painting artwork for 5 more hours...")
myPiece.paint(5)
print(myPiece)
print("What happens if I cook it for 2 more hours?")
myPiece.paint(2)
```

print(myPiece)

Your outcome should be:

>>>

Empty artwork.

Painting artwork for 6 hours...

Half-way done artwork.

Painting artwork for 5 more hours...

Perfectly finished artwork.

What happens if I paint it for 2 more hours?

Distorted artwork.

Hiding Data

There are two ways through which you can change or view the attributes inside an object. You can either access an attribute directly, by:

myPiece.finish_level = 6

OR

myPiece.paint(5)

The second method of modifying the attribute is usually used because the first allows for decreasing of the *finish_level*. Accessing the attribute means that you're changing at least two parts (the *finish_level* and the *finish_string*). Thus, we need a method that makes sure the finish_level doesn't reduce, but only increases.

Data hiding is the restriction of the access to an object's variable so you can just use it or change it by using methods. Python doesn't have a means of enforcing this data hiding, you can just write code that follows this rule if you want to.

There's just one more aspect of classes and objects that you need to learn, and they're *polymorphism* and *inheritance. You may have an idea what inheritance is, but there's a 90% chance you've never heard of polymorphism. Here's what they are:*

Polymorphism—same method, same name, but different behavior

Polymorphism means having two or even more methods that have the same name but are in different classes. As much as you may try not to, it's not impossible that this happens. You may get to use polymorphism a lot when calculating mathematics, especially in geometry. Here's an example:

```
class Square:

    def __init__(self, size):

self.size = size


    def findArea(self):
        area = self.size * self.size
        return area
```

```python
class Triangle:

    def __init__(self, breadth, height):

    self.breadth = breadth

    self.height = height


    def findArea(self):

        area = self.breath * self.height / 2.0

        return area
```

That's the formula for getting the areas of a square and triangle respectively. There's the method findArea in both classes. But they behave differently. When you add the print statement, you'll be able to calculate the areas differently. First, call the instance of each class.

```python
>>> mySquare = Square(12)

>>> myTriangle = Triangle(8, 10)


>>> mySquare.getArea()

144

>>> myTriangle.getArea()

40.0
```

Inheriting Functions

It happens on a lot of occasions that we get some traits from our parents, or even grandparents. And the higher the family tree goes, the more possible traits we can inherit. This is very similar to what happens in the programming world. You can have an object that stems from a class. And that same class could have been created from yet another class. It would happen that the functions that exist in the origin (second) class can be used in the first (object's parent) class and by the same token be applicable to the current object. Let's use our example of dog to illustrate this.

A dog is a *mammal*. Before it became a *mammal*, it was an *animal* first. And for it to be an animal, it had to have been a *living thing*. That's a pretty long family tree there. So, before you can get to the dog, you'll have to go through the long list first.

Living things > animals > mammals > dogs

The class that inherits (whether attributes or methods) from another class is called a *subclass or a derived class*. What this implies is that some of the functions in each subclass can apply to those in the object. Here's what an inheritance in coding may look like:

```
class LivingThings:

    def __init__(self, creature):

self.creature = creature

    def CreatureClass(self, classification):

# put code here to add the object

# to the classification's collection
```

```
class Specie(LivingThings):

    def __init__(self, name):

    LivingThings.__init__(self, "specie")

    self.name = name


    def family(self, age, colour):

        # put code here to remove the specie
```

To be honest, using abstract illustrations to explain objects and classes isn't all that fun. But the important thing is that you know the basis, you know how to create and use them, and you know how you can help your objects inherit functions from their class and subclasses. You already know that having the same object variable in the same class is an expensive game to play. You'll get a much better understanding of how to use classes and objects when you use them in real programs, like building games (which you'll understand as the next chapters).

Tips 'N' Tricks

- Class names usually start with block letters (like we used in the class 'Book'). It's not a rule, but it's just a convention that makes things easier for you and your code. Long live the programming tradition.

- Codes are getting even longer. But it's important that you type them all into your Python shell. You'd never know what you know or not unless you try!

- The Hashtag (#) – you may have noticed in the last code we wrote in this chapter, instead of inputting the codes we wanted the computer to process, we used a comment line to explain what should be inside instead and started the line with a hashtag. Often times when writing complex codes, programmers aren't always sure about what should be inside some functions yet. But they still have to write those codes. They employ this method. It's a way of thinking or planning ahead. These "empty" functions or methods (or whatever they may be in the code) are called *code stubs*. Although they aren't exactly empty, the comments written there don't add up to anything in Python language.

You may, or may not use a *pass* keyword while using code stubs. Using the keyword tells Python to ignore that code and jump to the next.

Chapter Nine

Python's Built in Functions

Asides being able to create functions, Python has some functions built in them already that you can just call up whenever you need them. They're referred to as Python's built-in functions. They make writing codes easier for you because you don't have to go through the trouble of making what's already made available for you. When we learned about modules earlier, we concluded that modules had to be imported before you can get the functions in them. Well, for these kinds of functions, they don't need to be imported first. You just call on them, and they are available for you.

Using this Built-In Functions

A number of functions exist, but there are some that every standard programmer has to know about and use from time to time. Let's check them out.

The Boolean Function

While we were discussing conditional statements earlier, we made mention of Booleans. We can now discuss them extensively. Whenever you're describing a data type that can only have two possible values, you're describing a *bool*. The possible values are usually True or False. This function takes only one parameter and always returns something based on that value. You can use numbers as your bool, and when the number is 0, it automatically returns as False. For other numbers, it returns True.

```
>>> print(bool(1))
```

True

```
>>> print(bool(0))
```

False

```
>>> print(bool(1123.23))
```

True

```
>>> print(bool(-500))
```

True

Strings returns False if there's no value for the string (having the keyword None or an empty string).

```
>>> print(bool(None))
```

False

```
>>> print(bool('yes'))
```

True

```
>>> print(bool('I bet this is going to be a positive string'))
```

True

Also, for lists, tuples and dictionaries that don't contain anything, the bool returns a false Boolean value. Here's an example.

```
>>> empty_list = []
```

```
>>> print(bool(empty_list))
```

False

```
>>> not_empty_list = ['this', 'list', 'is', 'not', empty']
```

>>> print(bool(not_empty_list))

True

A statement can either be true or false. The Boolean function is mostly used for conditional statements to determine if a statement is true or not. Take a look.

if True == True:

    print('everything is a lie')

The Eval Function

The eval function is short for evaluate. It includes just one parameter that it runs as though it were a proper Python expression. Let's try some examples.

>>> eval("12//4")

3

>> x=5

>>> eval("'if x==5:

        print("this isn't going to work")'")

The first code goes ahead to give you an output. The second, however, doesn't work. This is because the eval function only works for simple, single line codes. Anything more than that is too much for it to handle. Whenever you want to return what a user has inputted, it's usually advisable to use the eval function.

The Exec Function

This is the short form of execute. It's quite similar to the eval function. It's only more useful because you can run more than single lines with it. The exec function doesn't return values that can be stored in variables. The eval function does.

```
>>> first_exec_function = '''print('execute')

print('this')'''

>>> exec(first_exec_function)

execute

this
```

When you have programs that you need Python to read from files, you can execute (run) these kinds of mini programs. The exec function comes in handy when writing really complicated programs.

The Dir Function

While dir is short for directory, what it does is to provide information on any value whatsoever. A value can have different features that Python can explore in various ways. The directory makes up all the available information it has on that value to you. You may have a value that you aren't sure what it can do. The dir function allows you to quickly check and verify for yourself. Let's check some values out.

```
>>> dir('zone')

['__add__',   '__class__',   '__contains__',   '__delattr__',
'__dir__',  '__doc__',  '__eq__',  '__format__',  '__ge__',
'__getattribute__', '__getitem__', '__getnewargs__', '__gt__',
'__hash__', '__init__', '__init_subclass__', '__iter__', '__le__',
'__len__', '__lt__', '__mod__', '__mul__', '__ne__', '__new__',
```

'__reduce__', '__reduce_ex__', '__repr__', '__rmod__', '__rmul__', '__setattr__', '__sizeof__', '__str__', '__subclasshook__', 'capitalize', 'casefold', 'center', 'count', 'encode', 'endswith', 'expandtabs', 'find', 'format', 'format_map', 'index', 'isalnum', 'isalpha', 'isascii', 'isdecimal', 'isdigit', 'isidentifier', 'islower', 'isnumeric', 'isprintable', 'isspace', 'istitle', 'isupper', 'join', 'ljust', 'lower', 'lstrip', 'maketrans', 'partition', 'replace', 'rfind', 'rindex', 'rjust', 'rpartition', 'rsplit', 'rstrip', 'split', 'splitlines', 'startswith', 'strip', 'swapcase', 'title', 'translate', 'upper', 'zfill']

```
>>> dir(100)
```

['__abs__', '__add__', '__and__', '__bool__', '__ceil__', '__class__', '__delattr__', '__dir__', '__divmod__', '__doc__', '__eq__', '__float__', '__floor__', '__floordiv__', '__format__', '__ge__', '__getattribute__', '__getnewargs__', '__gt__', '__hash__', '__index__', '__init__', '__init_subclass__', '__int__', '__invert__', '__le__', '__lshift__', '__lt__', '__mod__', '__mul__', '__ne__', '__neg__', '__new__', '__or__', '__pos__', '__pow__', '__radd__', '__rand__', '__rdivmod__', '__reduce__', '__reduce_ex__', '__repr__', '__rfloordiv__', '__rlshift__', '__rmod__', '__rmul__', '__ror__', '__round__', '__rpow__', '__rrshift__', '__rshift__', '__rsub__', '__rtruediv__', '__rxor__', '__setattr__', '__sizeof__', '__str__', '__sub__', '__subclasshook__', '__truediv__', '__trunc__', '__xor__', 'bit_length', 'conjugate', 'denominator', 'from_bytes', 'imag', 'numerator', 'real', 'to_bytes']

As it is, there's a lot of things the string 'zone' and integer '100' can be used as that you may not have known about. It also gives you all the information in alphabetical order (Python happens to be quite orderly). There's practically nothing you can't use the dir function on. You can also try out something like this:

>>> direction= 'What direction do we go?'

>>> dir(direction)

['__add__', '__class__', '__contains__', '__delattr__', '__dir__', '__doc__', '__eq__', '__format__', '__ge__', '__getattribute__', '__getitem__', '__getnewargs__', '__gt__', '__hash__', '__init__', '__init_subclass__', '__iter__', '__le__', '__len__', '__lt__', '__mod__', '__mul__', '__ne__', '__new__', '__reduce__', '__reduce_ex__', '__repr__', '__rmod__', '__rmul__', '__setattr__', '__sizeof__', '__str__', '__subclasshook__', 'capitalize', 'casefold', 'center', 'count', 'encode', 'endswith', 'expandtabs', 'find', 'format', 'format_map', 'index', 'isalnum', 'isalpha', 'isascii', 'isdecimal', 'isdigit', 'isidentifier', 'islower', 'isnumeric', 'isprintable', 'isspace', 'istitle', 'isupper', 'join', 'ljust', 'lower', 'lstrip', 'maketrans', 'partition', 'replace', 'rfind', 'rindex', 'rjust', 'rpartition', 'rsplit', 'rstrip', 'split', 'splitlines', 'startswith', 'strip', 'swapcase', 'title', 'translate', 'upper', 'zfill']

It gives a list of all the available functions in the value. Because most of the things in the list aren't easily comprehensible to everyone, you can decide to use the help function to get an easier understanding of each. I'll pick a random function of direction and check what it means and does. You should do the same.

>>> help(direction.isidentifier)

Help on built-in function isidentifier:

isidentifier() method of builtins.str instance

Return True if the string is a valid Python identifier, False otherwise.

Use keyword.iskeyword() to test for reserved identifiers such as "def" and "class".

Usually, the last line gives a short description of what the function does.

The Float Function

A *floating point* number is simply a decimal number. This float function converts whole numbers (integers) to floating numbers. Let's try some out.

>>> float(18)

18.0

>>> float('16')

16.0

>>> float(334.66)

334.66

>>> float(05)

SyntaxError: invalid token

It converts the first three despite the second being a string of numbers (it still understood). The fourth doesn't work because the parameter is invalid.

You can use it alongside the input() function. Here's how.

>>> my_age = input('Enter your age:')

Enter your age:44

>>> my_age = float(my_age)

>>> age = my_age - 13

```
>>> if my_age > 13:

        print('You are', age, 'years too old')
```

You are 31.0 years too old

The Int Function

While float converts whole numbers to decimals, the int (integer) function converts strings of numbers to whole numbers. If you, however, try to convert floating numbers to integers, Python will be unable to. Here's how.

```
>>> int(123)

123

>>> int('123')

123

>>> int('123.45')

Traceback (most recent call last):
  File "<pyshell#212>", line 1, in <module>
    int('123.45')
ValueError: invalid literal for int() with base 10: '123.45'
```

The float isn't convertible because it isn't in base 10.

The Len Function

This function gives you the length of your string or the length of values in a list. If you need to know how many characters are in a string (including the spaces), the len (length) function is your go to. Let's try out some examples.

>>> len('How long is this example?')

25

>>> example_list = ['Python', 'IDLE', 'Interpreter', 'Compiler', 'Coding']

>>> len(example_list)

5

The first gives you the length of the characters in the string. The second gives the number of items in the list.

The Range Function

This function is one of the most popular, and we've used a lot before now. It usually has two (start and stop) parameters. It's frequently used for the two kinds of loops. What the start and stop numbers in the parameters do is to indicate where the loop (or any function) should start and the number to stop (just before). Let's try out some of the things we already know about range, again.

>>> for x in range(0, 11):
    print(x)

0

1

2

3

4

5

6

7

8

9

10

It sometimes includes a third parameter (a step) that you want to skip (step over) some values in the range. Some examples include:

```
>>> for x in range(23, 45, 3):
        print(x)
```

23

26

29

32

35

38

41

44

```
>>> for v in range(45, 23, -3):
        print(v)
```

45

42

39

36

33

30

27

24

The first starts from the first and steps over two numbers to show the third until it gets to the number just before the *stop* of the range. You'll notice that the second code displays every third number, only that it does it backward. That's because the step is in the negative.

The Sum Function

The sum in this function represents the summation. It returns the total of the summation of values. Here's an example:

>>> distance = (56, 56, 46, 122)

>>> print(sum(distance))

280

So instead of inputting 3 + (add up symbols) to give the total, the computer automatically knows to return the total value with the sum function.

The Max and Min Functions

The max function will always return the highest (maximum) value in a string, list, or tuple to you. In case you have to quickly check the highest number or letter in a string without having to look through yourself, the max function is useful. Here are some examples.

>>> print(max(45, 88, 97, 666, 111))

666

>>> print(max['gag', 'jug', 'loaf'])

Traceback (most recent call last):

 File "<pyshell#248>", line 1, in <module>

 print(max['gag', 'jug', 'loaf'])

TypeError: 'builtin_function_or_method' object is not subscriptable

>>> print(max('j', 'l', 'a', 'y', 'g'))

y

The maximum number in the first code was returned. The second was invalid because the computer couldn't pick out the highest value of the strings. You can't expect that the computer knows what the highest value is between a jug, loaf, or gag. But if you put a number of letters into individual strings in the third code, it picks out the highest value as 'y'. This is because Python reads the alphabets from the lowest (a) to the highest (z). Upper cases also come before lower cases. So, if you had a 'y' and a 'Y' in the list, the 'y' will still be the highest there.

The min function, on the other hand, checks for the lowest (minimum) value in the string, or numbers and returns them. Let's see how it works.

>>> print(min(43, 0, 22, 909))

0

>>> print(min('A','B', 'b', 'v', 't'))

A

Working with Files

Everything on your computer is stored as files. From pictures to documents to videos and games... they're all files. This will mean that Python is also a file in itself. So, since practically everything is possible with Python, we should be able to command our computer to open files with Python.

There's a built-in function, one of the most used (if I do say so myself), called the *open* function. Before you start asking Python to open actual files on your computer, let's create ours for the reason of learning. All computers have the **Notepad** program/file and it would be great to start with that.

On your Start window, find the Notepad program and open. Enter some random words into the notepad and save. Make sure you save it to the *C:* drive by double-clicking My Computer and clicking Local Disk(C:) twice. Save the file name as *testme.txt,* and finally, save.

If your computer is a Mac, click the ***Spotlight*** icon in the menu bar at the top of the screen and enter *TextEdit* in the search box that appears. Once it opens, type in random words in a few lines, and click Format and select Make Plain Text. Save the file as *testme.txt.* You click your username and click the **Save** button.

Opening Files in Python

Now that you've successfully opened a notepad file on your computer, we move on to opening it with the built-in open function. For Windows computer, you go through this process.

```
>>> test_file = open('c:\\testme.txt')

>>> text = test_file.read()

>>> print(text)
```

If you're seeing this, then you've successfully opened your testme file with Python

Way to go! You're always learning with Python. There's a lot more to learn.

There's a need to explain how this works.

We first create a variable that would be easy for us to use and ask that it open the file we just created through the open function. We inputted the correct location of the file, if not, it'll not open at all.

The second line uses the read function to read the content of the file and store it in the text variable. Remember, all these variables is so we can easily read, understand and recall the codes whenever we need them.

The last line is a command to print the content of the variable 'text' which in fact contains the file, which Python has read.

The output is going to be the random you inputted in your Notepad earlier.

For Mac computers, you open a file in a slightly different way. Here…

Use the same username that you used to save the text file. If your username is *tammydanny,* here's how the first line should look like:

>>> test_file = open('/Users/tammydanny/test.txt')

>>> text = test_file.read()

>>> print(text)

That's all you need to do to open files from your computer with Python. As you go on with your programming, you'll have to download or create some files on your computer and open them with Python. You can also decide to write to files from Python. Cool, right? Here's how.

Writing Files to Python

The open function can do more than just reading files. It has features to write files. Here's how to create files.

>>> test_file = open('c:\\myfile.txt', 'w')

The 'w' here is the part of the command that tells Python to write in a file instead of opening it alone. Writing more information in or empty file...

>>> test_file.write('If you're seeing this, you've successfully created a file with Python!')

>>> test_file.close()

The last line tells Python that you're done writing and, it should close the file. If you go to the file location on your computer and open it, you should see your input there already.

Tips 'N' Tricks

- All the words that represent the functions listed here, and more, means that they have a 'role' they're acting in your codes already. And because of this, you can't use them as variable names in themselves. Words like sum, max, float, and so on shouldn't be used as variable names. When you have long and complicated codes that you need to use these functions and they double as variable names, you're only going to confuse the computer (and yourself). There are a lot of words that exist today. Why don't you pick some of these words that Python hasn't yet assigned?

Chapter Ten

Random Fun and Games

At this point, it's safe to say that you've learned the basics you'll need to operate on Python. Way to go! You now understand variables, and all the data types that exist. You understand what it requires to write conditional statement codes, you know how to find your way around loops, you can calculate your math homework using Python, and you know what to do if you want your codes to look 'fancier' with GUIs.

Creating your own functions, using those already built into Python, and recalling your codes isn't new to you anymore. You know why it's easier to classify your codes and divide them into smaller chunks. You can even draw with Turtle. If you're confident enough that you can operate on and with all these sections, then there's hardly anything you can't do with Python. But if you feel there's something you don't really get yet, you should always go back to practicing on it. Even the best programmers didn't get it all right at once. Not to worry, you're on the right track.

One of the popular reasons young people want to learn to program is being able to create and build games for themselves and their friends. Well, you've learned enough to be able to build simple and exciting games for yourself. You can apply all your knowledge into making a game.

In this chapter, we're going to try recreating two already existing games. For the first game, if you love or like the idea of skiing, we can try a little, simple but exciting SKIER game. In this game, you ski down a hill, picking up flags while trying to avoid trees every flag picked gives you 10 points. But, you lose 100 points when you crash. Let's go!

Creating Your Skier Game

Skier (and a number of games) use a *Pygame module* to help create games for your game. The module comes with a Python when it's installed. But just in case you don't have it installed alongside your Python yet, you can get it from **www.pygame.org** right away. You'll also need some skier customized graphic files that'll be used for your game.

skier_down.png

skier_right1.png

skier_right2.png

skier_left1.png

skier_left2.png

skier_crash.png

skier_tree.png

skier_flag.png

They should be put in the same directory or path as the original program for easy access. Here's the code (that's a bit long, but not impossible).

```
import pygame, sys, random

skier_images = ["skier_down.png", "skier_right1.png",

        "skier_right2.png", "skier_left2.png",
```

```python
                    "skier_left1.png"]
class SkierClass(pygame.sprite.Sprite):
    def __init__(self):
        pygame.sprite.Sprite.__init__(self)
        self.image = pygame.image.load("skier_down.png")
        self.rect = self.image.get_rect()
        self.rect.center = [320, 100]
        self.angle = 0


    def turn(self, direction):
        self.angle = self.angle + direction
        if self.angle < -2: self.angle = -2
        if self.angle > 2: self.angle = 2
        center = self.rect.center
        self.image = pygame.image.load(skier_images[sclf.angle])
        self.rect = self.image.get_rect()
        self.rect.center = center
        speed = [self.angle, 6 - abs(self.angle) * 2]
        return speed
```

```python
    def move(self, speed):
        self.rect.centerx = self.rect.centerx + speed[0]
        if self.rect.centerx < 20: self.rect.centerx = 20
        if self.rect.centerx > 620: self.rect.centerx = 620


class ObstacleClass(pygame.sprite.Sprite):
    def __init__(self, image_file, location, type):
        pygame.sprite.Sprite.__init__(self)
        self.image_file = image_file
        self.image = pygame.image.load(image_file)
        self.rect = self.image.get_rect()
        self.rect.center = location
        self.type = type
        self.passed = False
    def update(self):
        global speed
        self.rect.centery -= speed[1]
        if self.rect.centery < -32:
            self.kill()


def create_map():
```

```python
    global obstacles
    locations = []
    for i in range(10):
        row = random.randint(0, 9)
        col = random.randint(0, 9)
        location = [col * 64 + 20, row * 64 + 20 + 640]
        if not (location in locations):
            locations.append(location)
            type = random.choice(["tree", "flag"])
            if type == "tree": img = "skier_tree.png"
            elif type == "flag": img = "skier_flag.png"
            obstacle = ObstacleClass(img, location, type)
            obstacles.add(obstacle)
def animate():
    screen.fill([255, 255, 255])
    obstacles.draw(screen)
    screen.blit(skier.image, skier.rect)
    screen.blit(score_text, [10, 10])
    pygame.display.flip()


pygame.init()
```

```python
screen = pygame.display.set_mode([640,640])

clock = pygame.time.Clock()

skier = SkierClass()

speed = [0, 6]

obstacles = pygame.sprite.Group()

map_position = 0

points = 0

create_map()

font = pygame.font.Font(None, 50)


running = True

while running:


    clock.tick(30)

    for event in pygame.event.get():

        if event.type == pygame.QUIT:

            running = False

        if event.type == pygame.KEYDOWN:

            if event.key == pygame.K_LEFT:

                speed = skier.turn(-1)

            elif event.key == pygame.K_RIGHT:
```

```
        speed = skier.turn(1)

    skier.move(speed)

    map_position += speed[1]
    if map_position >= 640:
        create_map()
        map_position = 0

    hit = pygame.sprite.spritecollide(skier, obstacles, False)
    if hit:
        if hit[0].type == "tree" and not hit[0].passed:
            points = points - 100
            skier.image = pygame.image.load("skier_crash.png")
            animate()
            pygame.time.delay(1000)
            skier.image = pygame.image.load("skier_down.png")
            skier.angle = 0
            speed = [0, 6]
            hit[0].passed = True
        elif hit[0].type == "flag" and not hit[0].passed:
```

```
        points += 10

        hit[0].kill()


    obstacles.update()

    score_text = font.render("Score: " +str(points), 1, (0, 0, 0))

    animate()

pygame.quit()
```

Try typing out your Python program with the right indentation. The whole code can be affected if you don't get it right. Most of the time, Python automatically helps you indent. But you still have to make sure they follow all the block code rules. The first step is making sure this code is typed in correctly, when you've done that, the rest is easy. Let's move to the next game.

Creating a Tic-Tac-Toe Game

This is a very common game that can even be played without a computer. It's sometimes referred to as the X-and-O game, and it usually requires two players (except you decide to play with your computer). For this exercise, however, we'll be creating one for two players. This particular game doesn't need any external or installed module to write the code. You can write it from virtually any Python code program that exists. Easy peasy! Just in case you haven't heard of the game until now, here's how it usually goes:

Two players are represented with the X and O symbols. Each player takes turns to put his symbol anywhere in a 3 by 3 game canvas. The whole aim is for a player to have this symbol appear three times either vertically, horizontally or diagonally. Each player tries blocking the other from getting this done. If, eventually, one player is able to get his three straight spaces, he wins, and the game is over. Usually, the game is played for a couple more rounds (until both players are tired) and there's a cumulative of who won the most rounds. If no one is able to get three straight symbol rows till all the tiles are filled, then no one wins that round and they move on to another. Tic-tac-toe is a fun game. Let's see how the code can be written.

```python
def tic_tac_toe():

    board = [1, 2, 3, 4, 5, 6, 7, 8, 9]

    end = False

    win_commbinations = ((0, 1, 2), (3, 4, 5), (6, 7, 8), (0, 3, 6), (1, 4, 7), (2, 5, 8), (0, 4, 8), (2, 4, 6))


    def draw():

        print(board[0], board[1], board[2])

        print(board[3], board[4], board[5])

        print(board[6], board[7], board[8])

        print()


    def p1():

        n = choose_number()

        if board[n] == "X" or board[n] == "O":

            print("\nYou can't go there. Try again")

            p1()
```

```python
    else:

        board[n] = "X"


def p2():

    n = choose_number()

    if board[n] == "X" or board[n] == "O":

        print("\nYou can't go there. Try again")

        p2()

    else:

        board[n] = "O"


def choose_number():

    while True:

        while True:

            a = input()

            try:

                a = int(a)

                a -= 1

                if a in range(0, 9):

                    return a

                else:
```

```
                    print("\nThat's not on the board. Try again")

                    continue

            except ValueError:

                print("\nThat's not a number. Try again")

                continue


def check_board():

    count = 0

    for a in win_commbinations:

        if board[a[0]] == board[a[1]] == board[a[2]] == "X":

            print(player1,"Wins!\n")

            print("Congratulations",player1+"!\n")

            return True


        if board[a[0]] == board[a[1]] == board[a[2]] == "O":

            print(player2,"Wins!\n")

            print("Congratulations",player2+"!\n")

            return True

    for a in range(9):

        if board[a] == "X" or board[a] == "O":

            count += 1
```

```
        if count == 9:

            print("The game ends in a Tie\n")

            return True


while not end:

    draw()

    end = check_board()

    if end == True:

        break

    print(player1,"choose where to place a cross")

    p1()

    print()

    draw()

    end = check_board()

    if end == True:

        break

    print(player2,"choose where to place a nought")

    p2()

    print()


if input("Play again (y/n)\n") == "y":
```

```
print()

tic_tac_toe()

player1=input("Player 1 enter your name: ")

player2=input("Player 2 enter your name: ")

print(player1,"is X")

print(player2,"is O")

tic_tac_toe()
```

Once again, try your possible best to input this code in your IDLE shell correctly. If you run it, and it shows error messages, go back to the line that has the error and make corrections. If doesn't, then you know you've done right.

Let's go ahead and get an explanation for the Tic-Tac-Toe, since it doesn't seem too complicated.

First, we define the game to include the board, end and win_combination elements. The board consists of a list from 1 to 9, which will eventually serve as the game board. The win_combination shows well, the possible winning combinations. There're eight of them. Under this defined function, we define another function draw that outputs the game board when we eventually run it. The next step is to define the elements of p1 (player one). You write a code that doesn't allow for a player to input his try on the spot where another player already has something. You do the same when you're defining a player too. Up next, you define another function that allows the user to choose a number between 1 and 9. If the number is not within the range, it sends a message that the number isn't available on the board. If the user enters anything asides a number, he is made to know that it isn't a number.

Next, you determine how a player wins the game, or not, based on the previous win combinations. If no one wins, the players are made to know that the game ends in a tie. The next set of code is that that instructs the different players at their turns to place their symbols. A special feature of the code is the last block that allows the different players to input their names for easy identification and more user-friendly. It also gives you the option of playing again if you wish, or else, it ends the game.

Running the code and playing the game is a lot of fun.

There are a million games in existence today. Some of them already put up their *source code* for whoever needs it. It's very advisable for beginners like you to search for this code, practice them in your own Python shell and see how the code works. With time, you get a hang of it and you begin to write your own codes (little by little) in no time.

The Unity game engine is a place to look if you're interested in making more games. It encompasses a number of things from physical engines, to 3D game engines even down to ways of writing game scripts.

Tips 'N' Tricks

- Some games require Python modules; others do not.

- The most common mistake made in writing codes (games or not) is the indentation error. You can go back to the previous chapters to see the rules that govern indentation in codes. If you can master the indentation rules, a large percentage of your coding errors and problem has been fixed.

- A *source code* is a code that holds the original of a particular program. It's like the person who first wrote the code's way of writing it. Over time, other users and programmers get to modify it and use it for themselves.

- Getting codes that are already available in public domains sometimes is a good idea. The only twist is you have to study it to understand what its programmer intended.

- There are a lot of ways to go about writing the same program. It's just the way it is. People see the same things differently. Two different programmers can write the same code in two different ways and still get the same output. It's the process that makes the difference between their codes.

- Remember, we're only at the simple, easy part of writing games. You can decide to change, modify these games, and make them look more professional. You can do this by enhancing your code. More on this in the final chapter!

Chapter Eleven

Game Programming

Putting your game code into a program is the icing on the cake for this basic introduction to programming (with Python). It's always an exciting journey with Python and code writing. I bet at the beginning of this book, you weren't sure if you were going to be able to get this far, but you did! Python isn't so tough to understand after all.

So, what exactly is game programming? Not once, not twice, but on a whole lot of times, we've mentioned programming at different points. Programming in its simplest form is making your codes into a program. All the lines of codes that you've inputted into your IDLE interactive shell will all come together and create a program that you can use on your computer or other gadgets.

Every icon on your computer, every app on your mobile phone, every game that exists is a program that was once just a bunch of codes written by someone. More often than not, you hear programmers say that the toughest part of being a programmer is writing the codes. It's what you do next, what you do with the code you've written. It may interest you to know that as much as making codes into programs is not as tedious as writing a good code, a lot of codes don't eventually become programs.

There's a lot of explanation for this. But top on the list is that most programmers are perfectionists. Until they believe the code is the best version of itself, they don't program them in the first place; talk less of putting it out there. But sometimes, you can't know what your code can do or what can be improved on it unless you try. It's very advisable that you always try to run your codes into actual programs when you can. If it brings up any problem, you're able to fix it. And if you're not able to, you may find someone who knows better to help you out. So, how exactly do we make our codes into programs?

For this chapter, we'll be focusing more on games. In the previous chapter, we wrote two extremely long codes for two different games. The Skier game, and the Tic-tac-toe game. And because the tic-tac-toe game could be run and understood even without GUIs, we ran the code and explained what each block and line of code meant. It's now time to do the same for the more complicated one –Skier game –and make into a program. Here's how.

We explain the code first.

- After importing the pygame, sys and random modules into our code, the next thing we need to do is create and program the Skier. This is done by creating an object and putting them into a Skier class with the *self* argument. There are five diverse images for the skier going down the hill. The variable angle (that contains values from -2 to +2) is also created to keep track of which way the skier is facing. The first value and image for going straight down, the next for turning left a little and another one for turning left a lot, one for turning right a finally the last for turning right little and a lot. At the start of the program, we made a list of these images, and we put them in the list in a certain order that the code follows. The value in variable angle is used to know which image to use. The value of angle is used as the index to the list of images. Skier_images[0] is the one used when the skier is going straight down. Skier_images[1] is the one where he's turning a little right. Skier_images[2] is the one where

148

he's turning sharp right. Also, we carefully use negative list indices (plural for index) where skier_images[-1] is the one where he is turning a little left (this would usually be called skier_images[4]). Skier_images[-2] is the one where he is turning sharp left (this would usually be called skier_images[3]).

- We make a class for the skier, which is already a Pygame Sprite. Since the skier is always 100 pixels from the top of the window, and we start him in the center of the window. Because the window is 640 pixels wide, left-to-right, x will then be at 320. This makes his initial position is [320, 100].

- Next up, you define the Skier to its turning terms and the method to move it back and forth. We make a class method to turn the skier, which changes angle, loads the correct image, and also sets the skier's speed. The speed has both x and y components. We only move the skier sprite left and right (x-speed). But the y-speed determines how fast the scenery scrolls by (how fast he goes "down" the hill). When he is going straight down, his downward speed is faster and when he is turning, his downward speed is slower. This block of codes doesn't allow the skier turn more than +/-2. The arrow keys to navigate the skier left and right, so we'll add our Pygame initialization and event loop code, which gives us a working program that only has the skier.

- The abs in that line of code gets the *absolute value* of angle. That is, we ignore the sign (+ or -). For downward speed, we don't care which direction the skier is turning, we just need to know how much he is turning.

- The move function created moves the skier left and right. This makes sure he doesn't go past the edge of the window.

- The anime function also redraws the screen.

- We go back to the main event loop and checks for key presses.

- At this moment in the code, you'll see just the skier without any score or obstacles), and you'll be able to either turn him left or right.

- The next thing point of the code is to figure out how to make the obstacles (the trees and flags). It's easier to start from the beginning again. But this time, there aren't any skier, just the obstacles. We've put the skier code together with the obstacle code at the end. The window for the skier game is 640 x 640 pixels. To keep things simple and prevent having obstacles too close together, we divide the window into a 10 x 10 grid. There are 100 spaces on the grid. Each space on the grid is 64 x 64 pixels. Because our obstacle sprites aren't that big, there will be some space between them even if they're in adjacent spaces on the grid.

- Once you've figured out how to make it, the code then start to create individual obstacles. A class is created for that, which now creates a single screen's worth of obstacles—enough to fill one 10 x 10 grid, which fills the 640 x 640 pixel screen. We randomly sprinkle 10 obstacles (flags and trees) in the 100 squares of the grid. Each obstacle can be either a flag or a tree. We could end up with 6 flags and 4 trees, 3 flags and 7 trees, or any combination that adds up to 10. They're randomly chosen (because of the randint. Function). Where the grids are located is random too. Since we don't want to put two obstacles in the same position, we should keep track of the places we have used and keep changing them. We use the variable location to indicate a list of the locations already used. We first check if a location is already in use before placing a new obstacle there.

- Next, the code keeps track of how far the map has scrolled up. If it has scrolled all the way onto the screen (at 640), create a new 'screenful' of obstacles.

- The animate function, again, redraws everything when the screen is filled.

- We go over the same process all over again and return to the main loop. The code keeps track of how far the obstacles have scrolled up and creates a new block of obstacles at the bottom. In your game program, you should see flags and obstacles scrolling up the screen. They just keep going up, above the top of the window, with their y positions getting more and more negative. If the game runs for quite a time, we end up creating a large number of obstacle sprites. But this could be a problem because of the computer memory. It could run out at some point. So, we need to fix things up. The update function we create helps us to ensure this happens. Here's how:

- It checks if the sprite is past the top of the screen. If it is, it automatically gets rid of it (self kill).

- At this point, we're nearing the completion of our game. We only need to be able to detect when the skier hits a tree or picks up a flag and keep track of the score and

151

display it. We need a function that detects when the skier sprite hits a tree or flag sprite. It will help us figure out whether it is a tree or a flag, and do the right thing. If it's a tree, it changes the skier's image to the 'crash' image, and deducts 100 points from the score. If it's a flag, it adds 10 points to the score, and removes the flag from the screen.

- The variable hit in this block of code tells us which obstacle the skier sprite collided with. It's a list, but in this case has only one item, because the skier can only collide with one obstacle at a time. So the obstacle the skier collided with is hit[0]. The passed variable is to indicate that a tree has been hit. This ensures that, when the skier continues skiing down the hill, he doesn't immediately hit the same tree again.

- We're getting really close. We just need to be able to display the score. In the initialization section, we create a font object, which is an instance of Pygame's Font class (it's in the Pygame's class already).

- The object font is rendered with the new score test in the main loop.

- The animate function is recalled again. We use it to display the score in the upper left corner.

And that's it! You have successfully programmed your Skier game right! You now understand the code in the last chapter better, you can now play your game with the Pygame window feature.

As a final chapter take home, here's some further experiments you can try with the Skier game and the entire Pygame module:

- Make the speed increase as the game goes on.

- Add more trees farther down the hill.

- Add "ice," which makes turning more difficult.

- If you're up for a real challenge, try adding a feature that shows your skier being chased by a random snowman or something similar in the Skier program. You'll have to find or create a new sprite image and figure out how to modify the code to get the behavior you want.

Tips 'N' Tricks

- To get more graphics knowledge on programming (because you'll need a lot when graphically representing your programs), you'll probably want to learn about something called the OpenGL, which is short for Open Graphics Language.

- It's always good to get to know other young programmers like yourself. You get to help each other and ask questions other people can't really relate to. You may have an idea of a programmer in your head as someone who sits all by himself in front of his computer without any friends. But a real programmer is someone who has a network (group) of programmer friends that help each other get the best out of their programs!

Conclusion

This is the end of this book and in turn, the end of your introduction to the basis of Python. If you've followed keenly through the chapters and have understood the rules and basis of all that has been taught so far, then you can proudly declare that you know and understand an important computer language. Truth be told, all that you've been taught so far isn't all there is to Python or computer programming. But it's all you need to learn to stand on your own and pick up what's left. Nobody ever knows all of Python totally at once, it's a very long learning process. It takes constant practice and consistency. Python isn't a subject or course you try out and leave for a very long time without trying your hands at (well except you've decided it really isn't for you). Let's highlight some of the things we've been able to discuss and learn so far.

- We learned what Python programming was and how to get started with the Python program. You definitely have what it takes to get a Python program running on your computer!

- Then we moved on to learning the various kinds of data types that exist. From strings (' '), to lists [], to tuples ( ), to maps or dictionaries {}. We learned how to put words, strings or sentences into different variables, how and how not to use them.

- You also realized Python can do your math homework and any kind of calculation you want even faster than your regular calculator can.

- We then moved on to *conditional statements*. These statements make you write codes depending on some condition. There're three kinds of conditional statements (ifs, elifs, and elifs) and just two kinds of results (True or False).

- Your knowledge expanded to loops. The for and while loops. You now they allow you repeat and iterate statements *as long as* something in there is true. Codes only loop when *something* in there is true.

- Then, an exciting feature was drawing different lines, shapes and graphics with the turtle module.

- Your graphics knowledge got extended to Graphical User Interfaces. You made codes look fancier than the regular old plain texts.

- We went to a higher level and learned about creating modules with various functions. You now know how functions behave and how you can recall them whenever you need them.

- We also learned to classify objects in our codes, as we'd need so we can 'stretch out' to them whenever we need them to.

- There're some built in functions that come with the Python program automatically. We learned that we didn't have to import them, as we'd do for modules. There are 12 major built in functions, with *open* on the forefront.

- For more excitement, we learned about writing codes for games and playing the actual games. Remember Tic-tac-toe?

- We finally learned what it meant to program games and other written codes.

After this, you may ask, what's next with Python and all I have learned?

Well, what you do next about Python depends on what you intend to do with it. Python is one of the easiest computer languages to learn. So with a good knowledge of Python, you can transfer it to learning other computer language. If there's one thing is sure, it's that you'll have to keep learning with consistency. Whether you want to major in game writing, or web programming or even data science, you'll still have to keep learning.

It would be a great idea to look for platforms where you can learn more stuff (especially with more graphics), meet new people, attend boot camps and just get better.

More Gaming?

For some people, they're already sure the game aspect of programming is what they'd love to explore. If that sounds like you, it's not a problem. There're a lot of books, materials, physical and online classes that are available for this option. Here are some:

- BlitzBasic (*http://www.blitzbasic.com/*), which uses a special version of the BASIC programming language designed specifically for games.

- Adobe Flash, a type of animation software designed to run in the browser, which has its own programming language called ActionScript (*http://www.adobe.com/devnet/actionscript.html*).

- Alice (*http://www.alice.org/*), a 3D programming environment (for Microsoft Windows and Mac OS X only).

- Scratch (*http://scratch.mit.edu/*), a tool for developing games.

- Unity3D (*http://unity3d.com/*), another tool for creating games.

You can also continue with the Pygame module (since it's a lot of fun) and create cool games. You can (should) also extend your knowledge on Pygame to make more professional games. PyGame Reloaded (pgreloaded or pygame2) is the version of PyGame that works best with Python 3. The pygame.org website provides a stream of practical tutorials for young learners.

Keep It Basic

A lot of books from as far back as when computer programming became a thing, there was a language referred to as BASIC popular amongst young programmers back then. It happens that BASIC versions have been made for computers today also. If you search and find them, they contain a lot of tasking games you can experiment on. You can pick a number of them and try rewriting them through Python. It's an amazing way to keep learning.

Other Languages

Python can take you a very long way, but it may not take you all the way. As technology is evolving, other languages are becoming very relevant. If you're convinced, you can go ahead to learn one or two more languages. But without any doubt, Python is the best language for beginners, especially young kids. As mentioned earlier, some rules that work in Python can be applied to other languages. Some of these popular languages are:

Java, JavaScript (they aren't the same), C/C++, C#, PHP, Objective-C, Perl, and Ruby.

Without any doubt, being introduced to Python is exciting and mentally tasking (in a good way), so whatever you decide to do with this new knowledge, make sure to do it well and never stop learning!

```
>>>print('Bye World!')
```

Made in the USA
Middletown, DE
10 December 2019